pocket posh® word power

(120) WORDS THAT ARE
FUN TO SAY

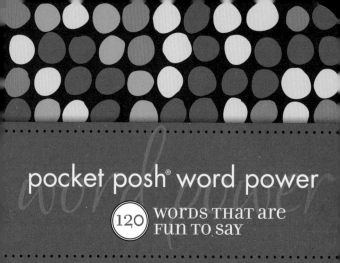

pocket posh® word power

(120) WORDS THAT ARE
FUN TO SAY

w♥rdnik®

Andrews McMeel
Publishing, LLC
Kansas City • Sydney • London

POCKET POSH® WORD POWER:
120 WORDS THAT ARE FUN TO SAY

Andrews McMeel Publishing, LLC
an Andrews McMeel Universal company
1130 Walnut Street, Kansas City, Missouri 64106

www.andrewsmcmeel.com

11 12 13 14 15 LEO 10 9 8 7 6 5 4 3 2 1

ISBN: 978-1-4494-1462-7

Library of Congress Control Number: 2010934823

Project Editor: Angela Tung

Illustration by robinzingone®

preface

When we think about words we tend to concentrate on their utility: Does this word accurately convey what I mean to say? Does it mean what I think it means? Will my audience understand me?

Even word-lovers concentrate on the more staid aspects of a word: the word's etymology, who used it first, its relationship to other words, and the range of contexts in which it appears.

Most of the time the pronunciation of a word is an afterthought, brought to mind only when the word in question is mispronounced. But here is a collection of words selected primarily for how wonderfully they roll off the tongue and how beautifully they complete the rhythm of a sentence.

Pick a quiet place and spend some time reading these aloud—soon you'll be leavening your sentences and adorning your utterances with such mouth-fillers as askance, cerulean, lollygag, and obstreperous.

absquatulate
/ (ab-skwoch'ə-lāt͵)/

verb

1 To depart in a hurry; abscond.
2 To die.
3 To argue (in the Midwestern and western United States).

Examples:

George St. George broke the silence. "We're not going to be able to absquatulate from these pirate yaps very easily, that's for sure. Guess we'll have to make the most of our stay here." —Michael D. Cooper, *The Runaway Asteroid*, 2004

Why, I expect in a year or two to see coffins introduced into the parlors of the Fifth Avenue, and to find them, when their owners fail or absquatulate, advertised for sale at auction, with the rest of the household furniture, at a great sacrifice on the original cost. —"A Day with the Dead," *The Atlantic Monthly*, September 1860

Coined around 1837 in the United States, *absquatulate* originated as a mock Latin word now mostly used in the Midwest and western United States. In the nineteenth century, a popular trend in American English was to add Latin elements to already existing words to create funny, pseudo-intelligent words. William Shakespeare did this

in many of his works, including *The Taming of the Shrew*, in which Lucentio poses as a fake Latin teacher to woo Bianca.

amalgamation

/ (ə-mal͵gə-mā'shən)/

noun

1 The act of compounding mercury with another metal. Specifically, a process by which the precious metals are separated from the rock through which they are distributed in fine particles, by taking advantage of their affinity for quicksilver.

2 The mixing or blending of different things, especially of races; the result of such mixing or blending; interfusion, as of diverse elements.

3 Consolidation; specifically, the union of two or more incorporated societies or joint-stock companies into one concern or under one general direction.

Examples:

The answer for the American auto industry comes in amalgamation—pooling what intellectual property they collectively have to develop the next generation of vehicles. —Gavin D. J. Harper, "Why the World Needs Green Motors, Not General Motors," *The Huffington Post*, December 7, 2008

In the Kedougou region of Senegal, the involvement of women and children ranges from ore extraction to burning amalgam, and in the Tenkoto region, the process of **amalgamation** is carried out by women, within the vicinity of their young children. —Onyemaechi C. Nweke and William H. Sanders III, "Modern Environmental Health Hazards: A Public Health Issue of Increasing Significance in Africa," *The Encyclopedia of Earth*, September 2009

Amalgamation cake, a dessert found in the southern United States, is named for its mixture of raisins, walnuts, pecans, and coconut.

anathema

/ (ə-nath'ə-mə)/

noun

1 A person or thing held to be accursed or devoted to damnation or destruction.

2 A curse or denunciation pronounced with religious solemnity by ecclesiastical authority, involving excommunication. This species of excommunication was practiced in the ancient churches against incorrigible offenders. Churches were warned not to receive them, magistrates and private persons were admonished not to harbor or maintain them, and priests were enjoined not to converse with them or attend their funerals. Also called judiciary anathema.

3 Any imprecation of divine punishment; a curse; an execration.

4 Anything devoted to religious uses.

Examples:

Do they not abound in anathema, and literally teem with the venom of intolerance? —Charles Southwell, *An Apology for Atheism: Addressed to Religious Investigators of Every Denomination by One of Its Apostles*, 1846

They are rich in anathema and maranatha of Brann's heartless and cruel detractors. —William Cowper Brann, *The Complete Works of Brann the Iconoclast*, 1919

Milk products are anathema to someone who is lactose intolerant. —Wordnik

Anathema was originally used by the ancient Greeks as meaning an "offering to the gods," often for evil purposes.

4   aposiopesis
/ (ap̩ə-sī̩ə-pē'sis)/

noun

- In *rhetoric*, sudden reticence; the suppression by a speaker or writer of something which he seemed to be about to say; the sudden termination of a discourse before it is really finished.

Examples:

Tamar's answer, "if thou wilt give a pledge until thou send it," is an unfinished statement, an aposiopesis, the omitted conclusion being, "I shall be satisfied." —Herbert Carl Leupold, *Exposition of Genesis*, 1942

"So . . ." said Mr. Carmyle, becoming articulate, and allowed an impressive aposiopesis to take the place of the rest of the speech. —P. G. Wodehouse, *The Adventures of Sally*, 1922

Aposiopesis is also applied to "the act of speaking of a thing while pretending to say nothing about it, or of aggravating what one pretends to conceal by uttering a part and leaving the remainder to be understood: as, his character is such—but it is better I should not speak of *that*."

5   appendectomy
/ (ap͵ən-dek'tə-mē)/

noun
- Excision of the vermiform appendix.

Examples:

It is estimated that, worldwide, more than 230 million major operations encompass a wide spectrum of complexity and indications, from emergency interventions (such as appendectomy), to lifesaving or life-extending operations (such as liver transplantation), to elective surgical interventions (such as total joint replacement), to cosmetic surgery procedures (such as breast augmentation). —David R. Flum et al, "Surgery and the Public's Health," *The Journal of the American Medical Association*, January 14, 2009

[Bret Michaels] the 47-year-old glam-rock reality TV star had an emergency **appendectomy** at a private care facility for diabetics last week after complaining of stomach pains before he was scheduled to perform at Sea World in San Antonio, Texas. —Derrik J. Lang, "Bret Michaels Has Massive Brain Hemorrhage, Rushed to Hospital," *The Huffington Post*, April 24, 2010

While Dr. Peppers was in training during the 1990s, the federal Medicare program was cutting back what it pays surgeons for many common procedures. For instance, in 2008, Medicare paid a general surgeon $562 for an **appendectomy**, compared with $580 in 1997. —Vanessa Fuhrmans, "Surgeon Shortage Pushes Hospitals to Hire Temps," *The Wall Street Journal*, January 13, 2009

While in the past, the *appendix* was thought to have no function, it is now thought it contains microbes that aid with digestion.

askance
/ (ə-skans')/

adverb

1 With disapproval, skepticism, or suspicion.
2 Sidewise; obliquely; out of the corner of the eye; askant.
3 To turn aside, as the eyes.

Examples:

Miss Douce halfstood to see her skin **askance** in the barmirror gildedlettered where hock and claret glasses shimmered and in their midst a shell. —James Joyce, *Ulysses*, 1922

The fox looked at the mouse **askance** from the corner of his eye; and the stoat could not refrain from licking his lips, though it was well understood that at these assemblies all private feelings were to be rigidly suppressed. —Richard Jefferies, *Wood Magic*, 1907

John looked **askance** at Tony when he suggested Mexican food for the third day in a row. —Wordnik

The origins of *askance* are unknown, but the word may be a variant of *askew*, an adverb meaning, "In an oblique position; obliquely; awry; out of the proper position or arrangement; hence, *askance*; sidelong."

baba ganoush

/(bä͵bə gə noōʹzh |

noun

- A Lebanese dish made from a purée of roasted aubergine, garlic, and tahini used as a dip.

Examples:

Also on the plate were roasted red peppers, kalamata olives, falafel (mashed chick peas with sesame) and baba ganoush (smoky roasted eggplant and seasonings). —"Greek Wild Iris a Treat in Tenn.," *BG Daily News*, April 23, 2009

The market, housed in a former Big Star grocery, also makes great homemade baba ganoush and their fresh minty tzatziki dip is so much better for dipping raw vegetables in than ranch dressing. —Chris Davis, "Pepper Paste at Mediterranean Market," *Memphis Flyer*, October 26, 2009

Such meals generally start with a selection of starters similar to those at breakfast, as well as mouttabal and baba ganoush (dips made with roasted eggplant), imam bayildi (eggplant stewed with tomatoes), kibbeh (balls of cracked wheat stuffed with meat) and a vast array of other dishes. —Sarah Irving, "What to Eat and Drink in Palestine and Where to Do It," *Matador Network*, February 4, 2010

Baba ganoush is Arabic in origin and translates as "father of coquetry."

8 **bafflegab**
/ (baf'əl-gab,)/

noun
• Slang for nonsense or wordy jargon.

Examples:
When all the bafflegab is stripped away, the decision to let Stanley Williams die is nothing more than George W. Bush logic with a Hollywood veneer. —Richard Wise, "Terminator to Williams: Hasta La Vista Tookie!" *OpEdNews.com*, December 17, 2005

"We've got to focus," says Lindsay, who is also the culture minister and—this is amazing—unlike many of his colleagues he answers questions you ask him and you can understand what the answers mean without consulting a translator of bafflegab. —Rick Bell, "Expo Man Says the Province Doesn't Have $1B for Either Calgary or Edmonton's Bid, but He Does Say Nice Things About the Capital City," *Edmonton Sun*, June 14, 2009

LaPierre's red-meat statements to pro-gun activists—cynical, incendiary bafflegab designed to anger up their hearts and open up their wallets—has effects that go far beyond the NRA's own political and financial interests. —Josh Sugarmann, "Scott Roeder: Latest Guy with a Gun Who Made the Rules," *The Huffington Post*, June 1, 2009

Bafflegab was formed by combining the two words *baffle*, "a disgrace, an affront, or artificial obstruction," and *gab*, "a jest, joke, mock, a piece of pleasantry, or idle talk, chatter, loquacity." Synonyms include *gobbledygook*, *gibberish*, *mumbo jumbo*, *double talk*, *double speak*, and *balderdash*.

9

bagatelle
/ (bag͵ə-tel')/

noun

1 A trifle; a thing of no importance.
2 In music, a short and light piece, usually for the piano.
3 A game played on a table having at one end nine holes, into which balls are to be struck with a billiard-cue.

Examples:
Every bagatelle—the one missing place card, the cloudy day, the tiny stain on the train of her dress—seemed like a disaster to the bride. —Wordnik

Should there be investors (nursed by Afghan opium dreams) delirious enough to sink their money into such a pipeline—

and that's a monumental if—Afghanistan would collect only $160 million a year in transit fees, a mere **bagatelle** even if it does represent a big chunk of the embattled Karzai's current annual revenue. —Pepe Escobar, "Blue Gold, Turkmen Bashes, and Asian Grids," *The Huffington Post*, May 12, 2009

The family felt a tremendous sense of relief. Here was assurance that Bobby was still alive. Merely for the payment of a trivial sum, a **bagatelle**, they would soon have Bobby back, safely home. —Simon Baatz, "Book Excerpt: 'For the Thrill of It: Leopold, Loeb and the Murder that Shocked Chicago,'" *The Wall Street Journal*, August 7, 2008

Bagatelle comes from the French word *bagatelle*, "knicknack, bauble, trinket," and is a diminutive of the Latin word *baca*, meaning "berry."

balderdash
/ (bôl'dər-dash) /

noun

1 A jumbled mixture of frothy liquors.

2 Senseless prate; an unmeaning or nonsensical jumble of words; trashy talk or writing.

verb

• To jumble and adulterate (liquors); hence, to mix with inferior ingredients; adulterate.

Examples:

One example of this **balderdash** is a lawsuit filed by Tapeshwar Vishwakarma, who represents a charity and claims that the human rights of the slum dwellers have been violated. —Alvaro Vargas Llosa, "A Bollywood Ending," *The New Republic*, March 3, 2009

How can you help being the mothers, daughters, &c. of Snobs, so long as this **balderdash** is set before you? —William Makepeace Thackeray, *The Book of Snobs*, 1848

Geraldine's mouth fell open as he proceeded to **balderdash** his jasmine tea with milk and sugar. Dealbreaker, she thought. —Wordnik

Duncan, of Cincinnati, mentioned as "delivering a dose of **balderdash**," is described as "the prime bully of the Kinderhook Democracy," without "perception of any moral distinction between truth and falsehood." —John Torrey Morse, *John Quincy Adams*, 1898

Balderdash possibly comes from the Medieval Latin word *balductum*, "to curdle or coagulate," or refers to *posset*, "a drink of hot milk curdled by wine or other liquor, formerly much in favor both as a luxury and as medicine."

11 ballyhoo
/(bal'ē-hoo̅)/

noun
1 Sensational or clamorous advertising or publicity.
2 Noisy shouting or uproar.

verb
• To sensationalize or make grand claims.

Examples:
Previous holders of the Olympic Games have found, once the **ballyhoo** is over, they are left with giant facilities having huge maintenance costs and for which local communities have little use. —Javier Espinoza, "London Looks to Learn From Others' Olympic Mistakes," *The Wall Street Journal*, June 22, 2010

In all the **ballyhoo** and attempts again to gain sympathy for Israel, Ms. Clinton seems to leave out the point that due to the Rothschild's continuing funding of the Nation of Israel, at the American taxpayer's expense in the foreign aid we have extended to that country since World War II, Israel has enough nuclear weaponry, power and might of its own to wipe the planet clean about 20 times over. —Betsy Ross, "Globalist Hillary Clinton Calling Now For Further Sanctions Against Iran," *GroundReport*, September 28, 2009

"Joan always likes to **ballyhoo** her cooking," said Margaret. "But really it's barely edible." —Wordnik

A *ballyhoo* is also a kind of needlefish that is mainly used as bait for offshore game fishes such as sailfishes and marlins, and as food in the West Indies.

12 **bamboozle**
/ (bam-bōō′zəl)/

verb

1 To use trickery; practice cheating.
2 To perplex; mystify.
3 To hoax; deceive; trick; impose upon.

Examples:

President Obama: See, I was trying to explain to someone the "okey-doke." Y'all know the okey-doke? It's when someone's trying to **bamboozle** you, when they're trying to hoodwink you. They are trying to hoodwink you. —Greg Sargent, "Obama on Veep Talk: Clintons Are Trying to 'Hoodwink' You," *TPM Election Central*, March 10, 2008

A tax plan where you pay a 27% federal sales tax on all retail purchases. Your paycheck will be free of all deductions except for health insurance and, of course, your state withholding but this bullshit **bamboozle** is a bait and switch scam. —David Glenn Cox, "Fair Tax: The Mother of All Dumb Ideas," *OpEdNews.com*, February 28, 2008

The dialogue between Don Manuel and Don Philip, in which the former undertakes to "**bamboozle**" the son of his friend, whom he conceives to be an arrant impostor, is absolutely a masterpiece of humour. —"Dramaticus," *The Mirror of Taste, and Dramatic Censor*, June 1810

Bamboozle is possibly related to the Scottish word *bombaze*, "perplex," and the French word *embabuiner*, "to make a fool of," or literally "to make a baboon of."

13 **Betelgeuse**
/(bēt'l-jōōz, *or* bet'l-jœz)/

proper noun
• The second brightest star in the constellation Orion.

Examples:
With about 15 times the solar mass, 1,000 solar radii and a luminosity 100,000 times higher than the Sun's, **Betelgeuse** is a star reaching the end of its life while burning the last remaining nuclear fuel at its disposal before exploding as a supernova. —"Betelgeuse, a boiling and magnetic supergiant star," *PhysOrg.com*, June 18, 2010

We may therefore conclude that the angular diameter of **Betelgeuse** is very nearly the same as that of a ball one inch in diameter, seen at a distance of seventy miles. —George Ellery Hale, *The New Heavens*, 1922

The surface of **Betelgeuse** is known to wobble in and out, fed in part by the roiling energy of convection beneath its surface. —Rachel Courtland, "Betelgeuse: The Incredible Shrinking Star?" *New Scientist*, June 10, 2009

Betelgeuse comes from a series of misinterpretations. Pre-Islamic Arabic astronomers named the star *yad al-jawzā'*, meaning "hand of Gemini." The ancient Greeks used the word in association with the constellation Orion. Scribes using Medieval Latin misread the word, leading to *Bedalgeuze,* which eventually transformed into *Betelgeuse.*

(14) **blague**
/(bläg)/

verb
• To humbug; boast; lie jestingly.

noun
• Humbug; vain boasting; pretentious falsehood.

16

Examples:

Jeff would often blague and boast about how much money he was making, but in reality he was thousands of dollars in debt. —Wordnik

Bertrand was opposite to him, and having listened with delight and reverence to some tale of knavery truly royal, was exclaiming with a look and voice expressive of the most intense admiration, "AH VIEUX BLAGEUR! va!"—the word blague is untranslatable—it means FRENCH humbug as distinct from all other; and only those who know the value of an epigram in France, an epigram so wonderfully just, a little word so curiously comprehensive, can fancy the kind of rage and rapture with which it was received. —William Makepeace Thackeray, *The Paris Sketch Book*, 1852

Blague is originally a French word meaning to joke or "talk through one's hat." The origin of the French word comes from the Germanic word *blague*, "bladder or pouch." The word *blagging* is used often in the Caribbean and means "informal talk, usually among men and in a public place."

15 blatherskite
/ (blath'ər-skīt,)/

noun

1 One who talks nonsense in a blustering way; a blusterer.

2 A good-for-nothing fellow; a deadbeat.

Examples:

When the people learn to distinguish between a hawk and a heron-saw they will drive this putrid-mouth little **blatherskite** from the pulpit. —William Cowper Brann, *The Complete Works of Brann the Iconoclast*, 1919

Perot, whose preferred rhetorical mode is the murky expostulation, is what used to be called a **blatherskite**. —George F. Will, "The Veep and the Blatherskite," *Newsweek*, June 29, 1992

Tom [to Roxy] "It's a thundering lie, you miserable old **blatherskite**!" —Mark Twain, *Pudd'nhead Wilson*, 1894

Blatherskite comes from a combination of the word *blather*, "a person who talks nonsense or to talk nonsense," and *skite*, "a trick, sudden dash, squirt: or syringe, slap, or a contemptible person." Originally *skite* was a Middle English word meaning "diarrhea."

16

blurb
/ (blûrb)/

noun

- A promotional statement (as found on the dust jackets of books).

Examples:

Asking someone for a **blurb** is the literary equivalent of asking them to help you move. —Matt Forbeck, "Blurbs: Billy Campbell," *Forbeck.com*, March 23, 2010

This is a novel featuring blog entries, essays, e-mails, newspaper editorials, extracts from interviews, even a **blurb** from a Guardian book review—a whole rattlebag of documents and contesting perspectives—and it fizzes with the effervescence a large book can have when its author is in total control of the material. —Joseph O'Connor, "Illustrado by Miguel Syjuco," *The Guardian*, May 29, 2010

That the **blurb** is a sentence fragment, not a sentence, is a clue that it's plucked from a sentence whose remainder isn't so adulatory. —Carl Bialik, "Is It Health? Wrathy? Toothy? Worthy?" *Gelf Magazine*, November 7, 2008

When he's not working, he loves to attend conventions such as the one this **blurb** is attached to, where he gets a chance to talk to fellow comic fans and buy even more art books that won't fit into his already stuffed studio. —"C2E2 Reveals Four New Guests of Honor," *Comic Book Resources*, August 21, 2009

The word *blurb* was coined by Gelett Burgess (1866–1951), an American humorist.

bourgeoisie
17 / (boor͵zhwä-zē')/

noun
- Properly, the French middle classes, but often applied to the middle classes of any country, especially those depending on trade.

Examples:

The struggle for money and a foothold in the Haitian **bourgeoisie** is unquestionably one of the principal forces shaping Haiti's authoritarian politics. —Peter Dailey, "Haiti: The Fall of the House of Aristide," *The New York Review of Books*, March 13, 2003

A political labour movement without deserters from the **bourgeoisie** is historically as inconceivable as would be such a movement without a class-conscious proletariat.
—Robert Michels, *Political Parties; a Sociological Study of the Oligarchical Tendencies of Modern Democracy*, 1916

Though not in substance, yet in form, the struggle of the proletariat with the **bourgeoisie** is at first a national struggle.
—Karl Marx and Friedrich Engels, *Manifesto of the Communist Party*, 1888

But, more than all this, I go on to show that the dominance of the idea of the **bourgeoisie** is a great historic move in the liberation of humanity; that it was a most potent moral cultural advance; that in fact it was the historically indispensable prerequisite and transitional stage through development out of which the idea of the working class was to emerge. —Kuno Francke, *The German Classics of the Nineteenth and Twentieth Centuries*, 1914

Bourgeoisie comes from the Old French word *burgeis* (or *borjois*), meaning "town dweller."

18

brimborion
[brim bôr'ē ən]

noun
• A useless or valueless object.

Examples:
Hortense [to the Chevalier La Corne]: Matter of **brimborion**, Chevalier! not to be questioned by laymen! —William Kirby, *The Golden Dog*, 1897

But amid the distracting and alien influences of bibelots and **brimborions**, the confused, contradictory, frequently completely unartistic, clamor and intercession of a multitude of archaeological objects collected from at least three quarters of the globe, and brought together arbitrarily and without the slightest regard for their own inclinations—

how can undisturbed introspective work be done in such an atmosphere? —"The Field of Art," *Scribner's Magazine*, April 1896

Brimborion may be French in origin. Its synonyms include *charm, gewgaw, trifle, bauble, knickknack, trinket, toy, kickshaw,* and *tchotchke.*

19   bromeliad
/ (brō-mē'lē-ad,)/

noun
- Any of various tropical or subtropical New World herbaceous plants in the family Bromeliaceae.

Examples:
The male frog then takes away the tadpoles that hatch, carrying them one by one on his back to pools of water which collect in **bromeliad** leaves high up in the branches of trees. —Matt Walker, "Peru Poison Frog Reveals Secret of Monogamy," *BBC Earth News*, February 22, 2010

Concentrating on the **bromeliad**, he strove to reach out and become one with the plant. —Frederick Barthelme, "Shop-girls," *Esquire*, 1982

This is characterised by low trees with thin trunks, with many **bromeliad** and orchid epiphytes; it grows on sandy nutrient-poor soils and averages 108 plant species per hectare campinarana or Rio Negro caatinga, a tall dry shrub-woodland mosaic restricted to the Rio Negro region which grows primarily in well drained uplands. —"Central Amazonian Conservation Complex, Brazil," *The Encyclopedia of Earth*, November 17, 2008

When I mention **bromeliad**, what is your first thought? Is it of a finicky, hard-to-grow tropical? Do you think it might be impossible to get it to re-bloom? If those are your impressions, I want to help you reconsider. —Norman Winter, "Bromeliads Brighten Holiday," *azcentral.com*, December 16, 2006

The *bromeliad* plant is named after Olaf Bromelius (1639–1705), a Swedish botanist.

20

brouhaha
/(broo'hä-hä␣)/

noun
• A stir; a fuss or uproar.

Examples:
In the middle of this **brouhaha** is the beleaguered Derek, who not only has to cope with the shifting moods of Sara and Chenille but also the debt he owes to Malakai . . . who took the rap years ago for a robbery he and Derek committed

together. —Andrew Sarris, "An Old Story: Her Husband Is Sleeping with His Wife," *The New York Observer*, January 28, 2001

Ironically, the biggest hit from that record, "Son of a Preacher Man," was thought by Springfield to be inferior to a version cut by Aretha Franklin just months later. Perhaps the **brouhaha** is a bit misplaced, but don't tell that to the dozens, maybe even hundreds, of female singers who worship at the altar of all things Dusty. —Darryl Smyers, "Shelby Lynne," *Dallas Observer*, February 7, 2008

The latest **brouhaha** is between Harold Bloom and James Wood (that's Yale against Harvard—without raccoon coats). Bloom says antisemitism is now rife among British intellectuals, and Wood replies that's merely one of Bloom's illusions, that the Brits are less antisemitic than Americans. —Dan Agin, "Harvard Against Yale in the *New York Times Book Review*," *The Huffington Post*, May 23, 2010

Brouhaha is French in origin and onomatopoeic, being imitative of the sounds of a stir or uproar.

21 bugaboo
/ (bug'ə-bōō,)/

noun
- A bugbear; a bogy; an imagined terror; something to frighten a child.

Examples:

This bugaboo is a big one: because Internet phone calls are made from an Internet "address" on a computer, and not from a phone associated with a physical address, 911 response centers throughout the U.S. are often unable to determine the street address of the emergency. —Russell Shaw, "FCC 911: Will the Feds Rescue Internet Phone Callers?" *The Huffington Post*, May 18, 2005

The hatching of the Dreiser bugaboo is here; it is the flat rejection of the rubber-stamp formulae that outrages petty minds; not being "good," he must be "evil"—as William Blake said of Milton, a true poet is always "of the devil's party." —H. L. Mencken, *A Book of Prefaces*, 1917

On commercial real estate (Eavis's main bugaboo) extrapolated losses are all of 0.9%, versus the government's adverse level of 9% to 10%. —Tom Brown, "Of Course Banks' 2Q Credit Quality Got Worse," *Seeking Alpha*, July 14, 2009

Earlier this month, we called the state-specific product code requirement "terribly unreasonable," and it would seem the state Legislature agrees, as lawmakers were already working on ways to remove this **bugaboo** from the bill. —"Disclosure of Fracking Fluids Vital," *The Daily Star*, May 30, 2009

An early form of *bugaboo*, Bugibu, a demon, appeared in an Old French poem, "Aliscans," in 1141. *Bugibu* may have Celtic origins.

bunkum
/(bəng' kəm)/

noun
• Senseless talk; nonsense; a piece of nonsense.

Examples:
Tall talk's his jewelry: he must have his dandification in **bunkum**. —George Meredith, *The Complete Works of George Meredith*, 1909

If any one were to ask him how people are to live within their means when they've not got any, he would reply with the word "**bunkum**" and clinch the argument with a grunt. —Stephen Hudson, *War-time Silhouettes*, 1916

But in recent days the government has stepped up its defense of the plans, with Prime Minister Kevin Rudd on Tuesday describing criticism of the tax as "**bunkum**" and "balderdash." —David Fickling and Lyndal McFarland, "Canberra Doesn't Retreat on Profits Tax," *The Wall Street Journal*, June 2, 2010

Bunkum comes from *Buncombe,* a county of western North Carolina. The congressman from *Buncombe* felt obligated to give a dull speech "for Buncombe" in the 1820s and the word came to mean any dull or meaningless talk.

23 **burgle**
/ (bûr′gəl)/

noun
- To commit burglary.

Examples:
He was wont to "**burgle**" the houses of the gentry round, and his favourite method of proceeding was to get on the roof and descend the chimneys, which in those days were wide. —S. Baring-Gould, *Cliff Castles and Cave Dwellings of Europe,* 1911

Ordinarily Spriggs was a cracksman, but the information he gained while at work one night so surprised him, that he forgot to "**burgle**," and then and there decided to get busy on a job that meant a cleanup of a $60,000 diamond. —Metta Victoria Fuller Victor, *The Blunders of a Bashful Man,* 1881

There was no rational reason to be creeping these halls stealthily like a thief come to burgle his own home—padding heel to toe on the floorboards, flinching when they creaked. —Lionel Shriver, "Book Excerpt: 'So Much for That,'" *The Wall Street Journal*, March 4, 2010

In the small hours of June 9, 1900, Simon Adams, a black farm laborer aged 19, was caught trying to burgle the home of his employer, E. H. Almond, who lived a little to the north of Columbus, in Muscogee County. —David Rose, "Excerpt: Seeds of Doubt," *Vanity Fair*, May 7, 2007

Burgle is a *backformation* of *burglar*, "thief." *Backformation* is the forming of a new word by the removal of an *affix*, "a word element attached to the front (prefix) or back (suffix) of the root word."

caoutchouc
/(kou'chook, *or* kou'choōk,)/

noun
- An elastic gummy substance, the inspissated milky juice of various tropical trees belonging to the natural orders *Apocynaceæ*, *Urticaceæ*, and *Euphorbiaceæ*. Also called India-rubber.

Examples:

A yellowish-white **caoutchouc** is now to be found in the shops, which may be easily distinguished from the dapicho, because it is neither dry like cork, nor friable, but extremely elastic, glossy, and soapy. —Alexander von Humboldt and Aimé Bonpland, *Travels to the Equinoctial Regions of America*, 1907

The plane trees contain **caoutchouc** and gum; peppers, ethereal oils, alkaloids, piperin, white resin, and malic acid. —Helen C. De S. Abbott, "The Chemical Basis of Plant Forms," *Scientific American Supplement*, December 10, 1887

Fritz and Jack were therefore dispatched to collect some fresh **caoutchouc** from the trees, and as this involved a good gallop on Storm and Lightfoot, they nothing loth set off. —Johann David Wyss, *The Swiss Family Robinson, or Adventures in a Desert Island*, 1882

Caoutchouc is more commonly known as rubber.

25

catawampus
/(kat'ə wəmp əs)/

adjective
1 Out of alignment, crooked, cater-corner.
2 Fierce, destructive.

noun
• A fierce imaginary animal, a bogeyman.

Examples:

Dear me, everything has gone **catawampus** with me this week. I spoiled the bread, as you know too well—and I scorched the doctor's best shirt bosom—and I broke your big platter. And now, on the top of all this, comes word that my sister Matilda has broken her leg and wants me to go and stay with her for a spell. —L. M. Montgomery, *Anne's House of Dreams*, 1917

Just check out spots like The Vig, located **catawampus** to the Arcadia district. —Steve Jansen, "Thank God It's Wednesday," *Phoenix New Times*, December 17, 2009

"Ninety-nine percent of the time, automation serves you well. You just want to make sure pilots can handle it when things get upset or the electronics goes **catawampus**," said one senior Southwest captain. —Scott McCartney, "A Radical Cockpit Upgrade Southwest Fliers Will Feel," *The Wall Street Journal*, April 1, 2010

After watching a horror movie marathon, Elizabeth was convinced there was a **catawampus** under her bed. —Wordnik

Catawampus as a "fierce imaginary animal" may be an alteration of *catamount,* "a wildcat; lynx; puma."

cerulean
/ (sə-rōō'lē-ən)/

noun
• A deep blue; a cerulean color.

adjective
• Sky-colored; clear light blue; blue.

Examples:

Now 745 Seventh Ave., festooned in **cerulean** blue, is the center of operations for the investment bank of Barclays, and there is no room in the new order for Mr. Fuld. —Heidi N. Moore, "Fuld Banished to Back Office," *The Wall Street Journal*, October 2, 2008

Patterns in **cerulean** blue, silver, and gray, with flecks of green and violet beautifully complemented the lunar gray visible through the windows. —Michael D. Cooper, *The Runaway Asteroid*, 2004

Our **cerulean** is very beautifully blue, but in Italy one discovers by contrast that it is an intellectual blue, filled with light, high, provocative. —Sara Jeannette Duncan, *A Voyage of Consolation*, 1898

In Paris nude statues are "draped in **cerulean** blue." —Sir Richard Francis Burton, Translator, *Arabian Nights*, 1885

In one of the principal rooms of the palace three beautiful females, clothed in **cerulean** robes spangled with stars, and their heads adorned with golden crowns, were at work together. —Benjamin Disraeli, *The Infernal Marriage*, 1904

Cerulean is related to the Latin word caelum, *meaning "sky."*

27

chiaroscuro
/ (kē-är̩ə-skoor'ō *or* kē-är̩ə skyoor'ō)/

noun

1 A method of printing engravings from several blocks representing lighter and darker shades, used especially in the fifteenth and sixteenth centuries; also, an engraving so printed.
2 Light and shade; specifically, the general distribution of light and shade in a picture, whether painted, drawn, or engraved—that is, the combined effect of all its lights, shadows, and reflections. Strictly speaking, however, every object on which light strikes has its own chiaroscuro.

3 Of or pertaining to light and shade in painting, drawing, or engraving.

4 A style of painting on enameled pottery practiced by the Italian potters.

5 A drawing in black and white.

Examples:

This difference in **chiaroscuro** is a more important character in water painting than mere difference in form. —John Ruskin, *The Crown of Wild Olive*, 1895

And that **chiaroscuro** is enhanced by some very funny moments in the movie; the director, David Yates, has lightened his touch since the previous installment. —Joe Morgenstern, "Latest 'Potter' is Long on Buildup, Short on Magic," *The Wall Street Journal*, July 14, 2009

The **chiaroscuro** is admirable: the impasto is perfect. —William Makepeace Thackeray, *The Newcomes: Memoirs of a Most Respectable Family*, 1855

Venetian masters made up the most heroic single project in **chiaroscuro**, and the 6 large landscapes, completed in 1744, after gouache paintings by Marco Ricci, were the most impressive color woodcuts in the Western world between the 16th century and the last decade of the 19th.

—Jacob Kainen, *John Baptist Jackson: 18th-Century Master of the Color Woodcut*, 1962

Chiaroscuro comes from the Italian word for "light-dark."

28 clamjamfry
/(klam jam'frē)/

noun

1 Persons collectively who are regarded with contempt; a mob; ragtag and bobtail.
2 Rubbish; trumpery.

Examples:

"If you put it that way I don't care one jack straw for the whole **clamjamfry** of them." —William MacLeod Raine, *A Daughter of Raasay*, 1902

Laird and leddies and bastards, the whole **clamjamfry**. —John Sillars, *The McBrides*, 1922

Miss Gillian, you've clavered as long as is good for Miss White, and here are the whole **clanjamfrie** waiting in the road for you. —Charlotte Mary Yonge, *Beechcroft at Rockstone*, 1889

"And what will ye do, if I carena to thraw the keys, or draw the bolts, or open the grate to sic a **clamjamfrie?**" said the old dame, scoffingly. —Sir Walter Scott, *The Black Dwarf*, 1816

Clamjamfry, also spelled *clanjamfrie* and *clamjamfrie*, may be Scottish in origin.

29

clodpate
/(klod pāt)/

noun
- A stupid fellow; a dolt; a numskull.

Examples:

Look at Arria worshipping the drunken **clodpate** of a husband who beats her; look at Cornelia treasuring as a jewel in her maternal heart the oaf her son; I have known a woman preach Jesuit's bark, and afterwards Dr. Berkeley's tar-water, as though to swallow them were a divine decree, and to refuse them no better than blasphemy. —William Makepeace Thackeray, *The History of Henry Esmond, Esq.*, 1852

The devil, you must know, came to the poor man's door, and rapping there, cried, So ho! ho, the house! ho, **clodpate**! where art thou? —François Rabelais, *Gargantua and Pantagruel*, 1552

Clodpate was most likely formed by the attachment of the two words *clod*, "a dull, gross, stupid fellow, a dolt," and *pate*, "the crown or top of the head."

(30) **codswallop**
/ (kodz'wol‚əp)/

noun
• Nonsensical talk or writing.

Examples:
In a 2008 book, Prof. MacKay dismisses what he calls the "**codswallop**" in the energy debate, such as government campaigns to get citizens to turn off their cellphone chargers. —Joseph B. White, "Climate Fight Heads for New Round," *The Wall Street Journal*, June 17, 2009

I was going to use the same description, but was not sure on the spelling; I was leaning towards "**codswallop**" though. —Melanie Phillips, "Creating an Insult to Intelligence," *The Spectator*, April 29, 2009

I would be interested to hear exactly how he thinks this would secure any future for mainstream media, when they demand that applicants hold the qualifications that these "**codswallop**" colleges provide, as well as experience. —Rachel McAthy,

"Now Is the Time to Make Your Own Opportunities," *Journalism.co.uk*, July 14, 2010

Mr. Packer, who has been married for over 30 years, said the allegation they had sex was "**codswallop**" and insisted he and his wife are the victims of jealousy and long-standing divisions in the Labour Party. —Nick Britten, "Lord Mayor's Husband Quits Labour Party over Sex Allegation," *Telegraph*, August 19, 2009

It is no real criticism of Sen. Clinton to say that she has not a snowball's chance in Hell of flipping TX (Obama has none either), but your hype here would make even the most ardent Obama partisan's blush at your effusive **codswallop**. —Eric Kleefeld, "Dem Congressman Walz Endorses Obama Because His Constituents Did, Too," *TPM Election Center*, February 6, 2008

Codswallop may have been formed by the combination of *cod*, which (among other things) can mean testicles, and *wallop*, British slang for beer.

31 colonnade

/ (kol̦ə-nād′)/

noun

- In architecture, any series or range of columns placed at certain intervals, called intercolumniations, from one another, such intervals varying according to the requirements of art and utility, and of the order employed.

Examples:

The scene from the colonnade is the most extraordinary, at once, and the most lovely that eye ever beheld. —Hippolyte Adolphe Taine, "Milan Cathedral," *Seeing Europe with Famous Authors*, 1914

At the end of the colonnade is a gigantic bust, representing a Hindu divinity with three heads. —Oliver Optic, *Across India*, 1895

The architrave of the colonnade is adorned with vases, connected together with festoons. —John Lewis Burckhardt, *Travels in Syria and the Holy Land*, 1822

So the itch to flaunt something, in the face of all this treasure and colonnade, is a time-honored one. —Christopher Hitchens, "Days and White Nights in St. Petersburg," *Vanity Fair*, July 25, 2005

Colonnade comes from *colonnato*, the Italian word for "column."

32

crepuscular
/ (kri-pus'kyə-lər)

adjective

1 Of or related to twilight; dim.
2 Active at or around dusk, dawn, or twilight.

Examples:

His eyes shone with quiet, greenish lights; from outside, the thin **crepuscular** light crept into the room through little crevices. —Boris Pilnyak, *Tales of the Wilderness*, 1925

The new-fangled deli has a smooth, form-and-function gloss, I suppose, but they lack the romance and magic of the crammed, cramped, **crepuscular** old-fangled delicatessen. —Matthew Fort, "Old Delicatessens and New Delis," *The Guardian*, July 12, 2010

Their "big-house literature," which blended descriptions of the social milieu of the ruling class with a nuanced and humorous appreciation of their society's **crepuscular** decay, includes marvelous works of art, such as Bowen's novel "The Last September" and Yeats's poetry from Coole Park, home of his aristocratic patroness, Lady Gregory. —William Birdthistle, "Behind the Green Veil," *The Wall Street Journal*, January 2, 2009

The primary strategy for dealing with high desert temperatures is avoidance—many mammals simply avoid the high daytime temperatures by being nocturnal or **crepuscular** (dusk- or dawn-active). —Peter Siminski, "Adaptations of Desert Birds and Mammals," *The Encyclopedia of Earth*, December 17, 2009

Crepuscular is from the Latin words *crepusculum*, meaning "twilight, dusk," and *creper*, "dusky."

33 **dandiprat**
/(dan'dē prat)/

noun
1 A little fellow; an urchin; a dwarf: a word of fondness or contempt.
2 A small silver coin formerly current in England, equal to three halfpence.

Examples:
And then she remembered, with a fluttering heart, that she was likely to become a great lady and the peer of this fascinating **dandiprat**. —Justin H. McCarthy, *The Duke's Motto*, 1908

"Well, miss, I guess you're not sorry to see an old friend's face, are you, now that the **dandiprat** redcoats you've been gallivanting with have shown that they prefer running

away to fighting?" was his greeting, as he held out his hand.
—Paul Leicester Ford, *Janice Meredith*, 1899

"He has won," he says. "How could he do otherwise? with
the plain truth on his side, and the Pope ready to steady
it on his legs again if he let it drop asleep. Arcangeli may
crow over him, as it is, for having been kept by him a
month at bay—though even this much was not his doing;
the little **dandiprat** Spreti was the real man." —Mrs. Sutherland Orr, *A Handbook to the Works of Browning*, 1927

Dandiprat was most likely formed by the combination of the words
dandy, "a man very concerned about his appearance," and *brat*,
"a selfish, spoiled child."

34

didgeridoo
/(diˌjərēdoōʹ)/

noun

- A musical instrument endemic to the Top End of Australia, consisting of a long hollowed-out log, which, when blown into, produces a low, deep mesmerizing drone with sweeping rhythms.

Examples:

The **didgeridoo** is a long, Australian aboriginal wind instrument, according to The Didgeridoo Specialists online. —Sonya Sorich, "What Is a Didgeridoo?" *Ledger-Enquirer*, April 7, 2010

Tuvan throat singing, like the (not dissimilar-sounding) Aboriginal **didgeridoo** is said to physically connect the singers to the spirituality of the Tuvan mountainside. —David McNamee, "Hey, What's that Sound: Throat Singing," *The Guardian*, June 2, 2010

Indigenous Australians protested that the routine was "very offensive," "cultural theft," embarrassingly juvenile, and that the **didgeridoo** was all wrong. —Maureen O'Connor, "And the Gold Medal for Most Racially Insensitive Figure Skating Routine Goes To . . ." *Gawker*, February 15, 2010

The patients who were instructed in circular breathing (as opposed to those who did nothing) and how to play the **didgeridoo** got improved sleep (and so, by the way, did their partners) and suffered significantly less from daytime sleepiness. —"Friday Weird Science: Snoring Problem? Have you Considered a Didgeridoo?" *Neurotopia*, June 25, 2010

Didgeridoo is onomatopoeic, or imitative of the sounds this instrument evokes.

discombobulated
/(dis͵kəm bäb'yə lāt͵əd)/

adjective
1 Confused, embarrassed, upset.
2 Broken, mixed up.

Examples:
His brain waves are still discombobulated from the liquor and none of what he is presently experiencing seems real.
—Steven Sills, *Corpus of a Siam Mosquito*, 2002

The singer proceeded to blow out the candles and spear the cake with his drumsticks due to his lack of a knife, followed by the crowd crooning a discombobulated rendition of "Happy Birthday." —Emily Singer, "Ringo Starr and His All-Starr Band: The Greatest Concert I Will Ever Go To," *The Huffington Post*, July 9, 2010

In court yesterday Mr. Roper described himself as "discombobulated" when [Senior Constable] Eather arrived because he had downed several glasses of wine and an unknown quantity of vodka. —Sarah Crawford, "Bizarre Defence 'Not Credible,'" *Sunshine Coast Daily*, April 17, 2010

One Cabinet member complains that the Kelly affair has "discombobulated" the backbenchers—instead of plotting to depose Gordon Brown, as they should be, they are worrying about their mortgage interest. —James Forsyth, "The Expenses Scandal Has Delighted the Tories—It Keeps Brown in Power," *The Spectator*, November 4, 2009

Discombobulated is probably a mock-Latinate word coined in the United States in the nineteenth century, based on words such as *discompose* and *discomfit*.

dollop

/ (dol'əp)/

noun
- A lump, scoop, or considerable quantity of something.

verb
- To apply haphazardly in generous lumps or scoops.

Examples:
There was the old farmer at the tithe dinner, who, on having some bread-sauce handed to him, extracted a great "dollop" on the top of his knife, tasted it, and said, "Don't chuse none." —Francis Hindes Groome, *Two Suffolk Friends*, 1895

In recounting his teenage travails as a Boston schoolboy growing up with a "dollop" of Catholic guilt and a full spectrum of FM stations, Sheffield navigates Reaganomics,

Boy George, and Rambo with wit, self-deprecation, and not an ounce of trepidation. —Kristi York Wooten, "A Girl Talks to Rob Sheffield about Duran Duran (and His New Book)," *The Huffington Post*, July 14, 2010

Now, with "Corduroy Mansions," set in contemporary London, he cooks up a delicious story that seems part Restoration comedy and part Victorian novel, tossed with a dash of mystery and a **dollop** of satire. —Eugenia Zukerman, "Alexander McCall Smith's 'Corduroy Mansions,'" *The Washington Post*, July 28, 2010

That left London with a large **dollop** of egg on its face. —Hester Plumridge, "Asia Leads Prudential Objections," *The Wall Street Journal*, May 6, 2010

Dollop may be related to the Norwegian word *dolp*, meaning "lump."

37

dragoon
/(drə-go͞on' *or* dra-go͞on')/

noun
- A cavalry soldier.

verb

1 To set dragoons or soldiers upon; persecute or oppress by armed force.

2 To cause to submit, as by persistent threats; compel by repeated acts of any kind; harass.

Examples:

Running to the window, I saw two men on horseback in **dragoon** equipments. —*The Atlantic Monthly*, Vol. 5, No. 32, June 1860

And when the horse receives a ball or a bayonet thrust, the **dragoon** is no longer good for anything. Have you ever seen a cavalryman on foot? It would be a pretty sight! —Edmund About, *The Man With the Broken Ear*, 1872

Their musical is about the writing of the musical for the festival, and they **dragoon** two friends (Jenna Sokolowski and Erin Driscoll), actresses trying to make it in musical theater, to be in the show. —Peter Marks, "Peter Marks on '[title of show]' at Signature Theatre," *The Washington Post*, April 20, 2010

Dragoon and *dragon* may sound alike, but they are actually unrelated. While *dragoon* comes from the French *dragon*, "carbine" (the rifle or a soldier armed with such a rifle), *dragon* comes from the Greek *drakōn*, "large serpent."

Elysium
(38)

/(i-liz'ē-əm *or* i-lizh' ē-əm)/

proper noun

1 The home of the blessed after death (in classical mythology).
2 A place or state of ideal happiness; paradise.
3 A region in the northern hemisphere of Mars.

adjective

1 Blissful; euphoric.
2 Of or pertaining to Elysium.

Examples:

The Greeks also believed in an **Elysium**—some distant island of the ocean, ever cooled by refreshing breezes, and where spring perpetual reigned—to which, after death, the blessed were conveyed, and where they were permitted to enjoy it happy destiny. —Marcius Willson and Robert Pierpont Wilson, *Mosaics of Grecian History*, 1883

By comparison to the ghostly condition of the shades in Hades, a full-bodied existence in **Elysium** is enviable, to be sure, if only because happiness outside of the body is very difficult for human beings to imagine and impossible for them to desire. —Robert Pogue Harrison, "Gardens: An Essay on the Human Condition," *The Wall Street Journal*, June 6, 2008

The French have a soup which they call "Potage a la Camerani" of which it is said "a single spoonful will lap the palate in **Elysium**; and while one drop remains on the tongue, each other sense is eclipsed by the voluptuous thrilling of the lingual nerves!" —"The Diligence: A Leaf from a Journal," *The Mirror of Literature, Amusement, and Instruction*, October 25, 1828

Elysium is often used synonymously with *heaven*.

39

eschatology
/ (es̩kə-tol'ə-jē)/

noun

1 System of doctrines concerning final matters, such as death.

2 The study of the end times—the end of the world, notably in Christian theology the second coming of Christ, the Apocalypse or the Last Judgment.

Examples:

The study of last things is called **eschatology** from the Greek word *eschatos*, meaning "the last or extreme." —"Catholic Biblical Apologetics," *Free Republic*, May 15, 2010

The subject of **eschatology** is so vast that it is hopeless to deal with it, even in the most summary fashion, in one paragraph. —W. R. Inge, "Religion," *The Legacy of Greece*, 1921

So ineffective is the current eschatology, in its bearing on conduct, that the latent energy of Man's nature—his latent desire to have a central purpose in life—is compelling him to work out for himself another and a more mundane conception of salvation, to set before himself at the end of life the winning of certain temporal prizes, and to keep this end steadily in view from day to day and from year to year. —Edmond Holmes, *What Is and What Might Be*, 1912

Eschatology is literally the "speaking or treating of" (from the Greek *-logia* or *-logos*) *eschaton*, the "day at the end of time."

40

eucalyptus
/ (yo͞oˌkə-lip'təs)/

noun

- An important genus of myrtaceous evergreen trees and shrubs, including about 120 species, abundant in all parts of Australia, and occurring rarely in New Guinea, Timor, and the Moluccas.

Examples:

Broad-headed snakes live in eucalyptus forests in the vicinity of Sydney, where they take refuge under thin slabs of rock atop sandstone plateaus. —Todd Palmer and Rob Pringle, "Slash and Burn to Save Endangered Species?" *The Huffington Post*, March 30, 2009

The alcoholic tincture of **eucalyptus** is useful in malarious regions (as are all the alcoholics, beginning with wine) in quickening the circulation of the blood; may it, perhaps, also act as a preservative against light attacks of malaria?
—Conrad Tommasi Crudeli, "Malaria," *Scientific American Supplement*, October 11, 1884

Now the smell of clean has become a wildly varied bouquet: mandarin-lime detergent, disinfectant evoking "lavender vanilla and comfort," toilet-bowl cleaner in **eucalyptus** mint. —Ellen Byron, "Is the Smell of Moroccan Bazaar Too Edge for American Homes?" *The Wall Street Journal*, February 3, 2009

Eucalyptus comes from the Greek *eu*, "well," and *kalyptos*, "covered."

fandangle
/(fan dang'l)/

noun
• A fancy or outlandish trinket or ornament.

Examples:
"Tish is changed, Lizzie," Aggie said hollowly. "Ask her for bread these days and she gives you a Cluny-lace **fandangle**. On mother's anniversary she sent me a set of doilies; and when Charlie Sands was in the hospital with appendicitis

she took him a pair of pillow shams. It's that Syrian!" —Mary Roberts Rinehart, *Tish*, 1916

Mrs. Greene [to Patty]: "And I'll come, and be awful glad of the chance! Why, I've never had a ride in a motor 64 car in my life, and I've never eaten in one of those **fandangle** hotels; and the way you put it, I'm just crazy to go!" —Carolyn Wells, *Patty's Social Season*, 1913

It is the question which will have crossed the minds of Gianluigi Buffon, Kaka, perhaps David Villa, in these crazy past four months and the answer most people might give will include apartments, Ferraris and all the other trappings which come with the whole Arab ownership **fandangle**. —Ian Herbert, "The Kompany That You Keep," *The Independent*, January 10, 2009

Fandangle may be an alteration of *fandango*, a kind of Spanish dance or music, or "an unknown entity or contraption," and the two words are often used interchangeably.

42

fichu

/ (fish'ōō *or* fē-shōō')/

noun

- A small triangular piece of stuff; hence, any covering for the neck and shoulders forming part of a woman's dress, sometimes a small light covering, as of lace or muslin.

Examples:

In her simple white dress, cut away at the throat, with a soft muslin fichu tied in front with long ends falling to the bottom other skirt, she looked, as old Macdonald afterwards remarked to his wife, "as a lady should:" fair, and fresh, and young. —H. Louisa Bedford, *The Village by the River*, 1910

It is curious to see the two portraits of the same epoch so absolutely unlike. Mme. de Chavagnac, an old lady, very simply dressed, almost Puritanical, with a white muslin fichu over her plain black silk dress—the other, Mademoiselle de Lafayette, in the court dress of the time of Louis XVI, pearls and roses in the high, powdered coiffure and a bunch of orange flowers on one shoulder, to indicate that she was not a married woman. —Mary King Waddington, *Chateau and Country Life in France*, 1909

The first was a positive matter of morality—it was quite improper not to wear a fichu; the second was the ensign of a good housewife—she appeared to think that by means of it she somehow effected a large saving in her brother's income. —Charlotte Brontë, *Shirley*, 1849

In French *fichu* means "put together, dressed up," and comes from the word *ficher*, meaning "to fix."

43

fiddle-faddle
/ (fid'l-fad¦l)/

verb
- To trifle; busy one's self with nothing; talk trifling nonsense; dawdle; dally.

noun
1 Trifling talk; trifles.
2 Trifling; making a bustle about nothing.

Examples:
She drove over constantly from Roehampton and entertained her friend with faint fashionable fiddle-faddle and feeble Court slip-slop. —William Makepeace Thackeray, *Vanity Fair*, 1848

Unfettered by chapter divisions or other organizational fiddle-faddle, the Cuban expatriate writer (himself a beatifically complacent cigar smoker) celebrates tobacco in a blithely disjointed monologue: the ramblings of a cheerful Pooh-Bah who is scholar and groupie, poet and stand-up comic and guru, all in one. —Josh Rubins, "Puffs," *The New York Review of Books*, May 8, 1986

Fraser, who once described Watts as a fellow "of some talent in writing verses on children dying of colic, and a skill in putting together **fiddle-faddle** fooleries, which look pretty in print; in other respects of an unwashed appearance; no particular principles, with well-bitten nails, and a great genius for back-biting." —"Authors and Books," *The International Monthly*, April 1851

Fiddle-faddle is a *reduplication*—"the repeating of a word or section of a word in order to form a new word or phrase, possibly with modification of one of the repetitions"—of *fiddle*, "to play aimlessly."

filibuster
/ (fil'ə-bus͵tər)/

noun

1 A freebooter, or mercenary soldier.
2 Delaying tactics, especially long, often irrelevant speeches given in order to delay progress or the making of a decision, especially on the floor of the U.S. Senate.
3 A member of a legislative body causing such obstruction.

verb

1 To take part in a private military action in a foreign country.

2 To use obstructionist tactics in a legislative body.

Examples:

The term **filibuster** traces back to the Spanish word *filibustero* or pirate (itself derived from the Dutch *vrijbuiter* or freebooter) and refers to the capacity of obstructionist legislators to hijack or "pirate" legislative debate. —Jerome Karabel, "Bring Back the Cots! The Filibuster and Health Care Reform," *The Huffington Post*, November 18, 2009

That may seem like a radical change, but recall that the **filibuster** is an accident, and there is nothing radical or strange about majority voting: we use it for elections (Scott Brown won with 51 percent of the vote, not 60 percent), Supreme Court decisions, and the House of Representatives. —"What Happens When Congress Fails to Do Its Job?" *Newsweek*, March 27, 2010

Terry's main concern is that Republicans will "refuse" to **filibuster** Sotomayor—which, without one Democratic Senator refusing to support cloture, they can't. —Megan Carpentier, "Operation Rescue Goes Predictably Negative, Crazy on Sotomayor," *Jezebel*

Filibusters originally referred to members of mid-nineteenth century revolutionary expeditions, such as those led by Narcisco López from New Orleans against Cuba and by William Walker from California against Sonora, a Mexican state, and Nicaragua.

45 fisticuffs
/(fis'ti-kufs͵)/

noun

1 An impromptu fight with the fists, usually between only two people.
2 Bare-knuckled boxing, a form of boxing done without boxing gloves or similar padding.

Examples:

There will undoubtedly be those who will rise before day break on Black Friday, bowing at the alter of consumerism, arriving at an ungodly hour, ignoring the humanity of others, some may even engage in **fisticuffs,** in order to allegedly save a few dollars. —Byron Williams, "Finding That Reason To Be Thankful," *The Huffington Post*, November 25, 2009

Without players who specialized in **fisticuffs,** a team's star players would be beaten to a pulp. —Reed Albergotti, "Why the Red Wings Don't Fight," *The Wall Street Journal*, April 15, 2009

The very next day, a cyclist blew a red light and slammed into a pickup truck, which sent the biker to the hospital. The day after that, Adam Leckie and Patrick Schrepping wound up in fisticuffs over Schrepping's admonition to Leckie for riding around helmetless. —Winston Ross, "Pedal vs. Metal," *Newsweek*, July 28, 2008

Fisticuffs is made up of *fisty*, "with the fists," and *cuff*, "to strike with an open hand; to fight; scuffle."

46 flapdoodle
/(flap dōōd'l)/

noun
1 Nonsense.
2 Speakers and writers of nonsense.

Examples:
Now you could criticize Barack for making too much of his insight as even I knew—at the time—that the administration was full of blather and flapdoodle—and I did not get any of the data that was available to members of the Armed services members of the senate. —Susan Rice, "C'Mon, Senators Clinton and McCain," *The Huffington Post*, March 6, 2008

A wire-service critic, William Ewald, called the show an "essay in flummery and flapdoodle" and complained about the woman who said her crippled husband was unemployed, her baby's lungs had been scarred by pneumonia, "and, rather anticlimactically I thought, she added that she and her husband both had astigmatism." —Cynthia Crossen, "Reality Shows Today Evolved From Contest of Competing Misery," *The Wall Street Journal*, February 4, 2008

Flapdoodle was known as "the stuff on which fools are feigned to be nourished," and may have originated in Frederick Marryat's book, *Peter Simple* (1873).

47

flibbertigibbet
/ (flib'ər-tē-jib,it)/

noun
1 An offbeat, skittish person; especially said of a young woman.
2 An imp, a fiend.
3 A flighty person; someone regarded as silly, irresponsible, or scatterbrained, especially someone who chatters or gossips.

Examples:
There are certain women who are a form of insurance to a man; and Anne gave a poise and solidity to Julian's presentation of himself which his own flibbertigibbet manner made particularly necessary. —Alice Duer Miller, "Slow Poison," *O. Henry Memorial Award Prize Stories of 1920*

Oh, can't you understand that I know you are worthless, and that you have never loved any human being in all your life except that **flibbertigibbet** Stella Blagden, and that I know, too, you have so rarely failed me! —James Branch Cabell, *The Cords of Vanity*, 1929

Or does it not rather suggest that Moll is such a **flibbertigibbet** that her religious views change with every new protector? —Ronald Paulson, "Reading Hogarth," *The New York Review of Books*, August 12, 1993

He suggested that the [Prime Minister]'s often tired appearance might be an advantage compared to Conservative leader David Cameron, who he dismissed as a "**flibbertigibbet**." —"Mandleson Slams Brown Pill Rumours," *Somerset County Gazette*, September 28, 2009

Flibbertigibbet is probably imitative of gossips' chattery nonsense.

48

fortuitous
/ (fôr-tōō'i-təs *or* fôr-tyōō'i-təs)/

adjective
- Accidental; casual; happening by chance; coming or occurring without any cause, or without any general cause; random.

Examples:

Connection of thought, even though purely fortuitous, is taken to indicate actual connection of the things represented in thought. —Edwin Sidney Hartland, *The Science of Fairy Tales*, 1891

These movements are not in fortuitous or chaotic ways, but are doubtless in accordance with some perfect plan. —Henry White Warren, *Recreations in Astronomy*, 1895

In the second chapter of that work, Darwin observes that small "fortuitous" variations in individual organisms, though of small interest to the systematist, are of the "highest importance" for his theory, since these minute variations often confer on the possessor of them, some advantage over his fellows in the quest for the necessaries of life. —E. Dennert, *At the Deathbed of Darwinism*, 1904

In 2003 and early 2004, a couple things happened—not planned, kind of fortuitous—that started the site off on the path to where it is today. —Jeff Cohen, "Josh Marshall on the Growth of Talking Points Memo and Independent Media," *The Huffington Post*, October 3, 2008

Fortuitous is often used incorrectly to mean "lucky," while in actuality, the word describes events neither lucky nor unlucky but simply random.

49 fracas

/ (frā'kəs *or* frak'əs)/

noun

- A disorderly noise or uproar; a brawl or noisy quarrel; a disturbance.

Examples:

[J]ust as soon as this fracas is over, when you know that we were right and that all this is a put-up job on you, your friend Trevors playing you for a sucker and getting Miss Sanford out of the way, you'll say we were right and I know it. —Jackson Gregory, *Judith of Blue Lake Ranch*, 1919

The political threshold that Senate Democrats established in this fracas is a measure of how distorted their antiterror priorities have become. —"Schumer's Epiphany," *The Wall Street Journal*, November 5, 2007

And their brawl, in a Buddhist temple with stone statues that get smashed in the fracas, is well worth seeing, even if the stars [Jet Li and Jackie Chan] now 43 and 54, respectively, are no longer in their primes athletically or onscreen. —Alex Remington, "*The Forbidden Kingdom*: Bad Script, Bad Acting, Bad Score, Otherwise Okay Movie," *The Huffington Post*, April 19, 2008

The Leno–O'Brien **fracas** is both shocking—an explosion of incivility that burns through late-night bonhomie—and also reassuring. —Alessandra Stanley, "Where's Johnny? Good Manners Take Hiatus," *The New York Times*, January 21, 2010

Fracas comes from the Latin word *fracassare*, meaning "to smash or shatter into pieces," which contains the root, *quassare*, "to shake, shatter." *Fricassee*, a dish composed of poultry or other meat cut into small pieces—in a way, "shattered"—was also formed from *quassare*.

50 furphy
/(fûr'fē)/

noun
• A rumor, or an erroneous or improbable story.

Examples:
Mind you, the "dangers of mobile phones" **furphy** is the mere tip of the iceberg. Also out in my neck of the woods are a family who will not have their kids vaccinated against common childhood diseases because of their fear of the little precious snowflakes being poisoned by the vaccines, despite almost no evidence indicating such is any sort of common occurrence. —"Pseudoscience Kills," *Machine Gun Keyboard*, January 11, 2009

He completely swallowed the **furphy** that demand deficiency and hence lack of spending is what kept unemployment at an abominable level during the 1930s. Now economic theory clearly states that if any factor, including labour, is paid for any reason in excess of the value of its product, a surplus must emerge. —Gerard Jackson, "Why Bernanke's Theories on Inflation and Unemployment Are Mistaken," *Seeking Alpha*, February 4, 2009

Next day, Chanel skipped back to America, where media outlets gleefully seized on the London **furphy** [false report], without checking the facts. —Eric Shackle, "The Secrets to Long Life From One of the World's Oldest Dogs (Eat Kangaroos and Emus)," *K9 Magazine*, March 9, 2009

Furphy is Australian in origin.

 51

galimatias
/ (gal͵ə-mā'shē-əs *or* gal͵ə-mat'ē-əs)/

noun
1 Confused talk; gibberish; nonsense of any kind.
2 Any confused or nonsensical mixture of incongruous things.

Examples:

I have seen this letter in which you tell me there is so much **galimatias**, and I assure you that I have not found any at all. On the contrary, I find everything very plainly expressed . . . —Nathan Sheppard, *The Essays of "George Eliot,"* 1883

He goes on with an eternal **galimatias** of patriotism, with such a self-sufficient air and decided tone! never suspecting that he says only what other people make him say, and that he is listened to, only to find out what *some people* think. —Maria Edgeworth, *Tales and Novels*, 1857

Some of the **galimatias** regarding Sotomayor's identity has to do with lack of understanding of Puerto Rico's confused legal status. —Gregg Easterbrook, "What Is the 'National Origin' of Apple Pie?" *The Huffington Post*, May 29, 2009

Galimatias is French in origin, and may come from *galimafrée*—in English, *gallimaufry*, "a medley"—which is a French sauce or ragout. The word was formed by combining *galer*, "to make merry," and *mafrer*, "to gorge on food."

52 glockenspiel

/ (glok'ən-spēl, *or* glok'ən-shpēl) /

noun

- A musical instrument consisting of a series of small bells or metal rods or tubes, mounted in a frame and struck by hammers; sometimes the latter are manipulated from a keyboard.

Examples:

Like the celeste, the glockenspiel is also made of metal plates; however, instead of the metal plates being struck by hammers, they are struck by hard metal mallets held by you, the player, like a xylophone. —Tracy Katz, "Modartt Celeste Add-On Instrument For Pianoteq Released," *Gearwire*, July 1, 2010

But through the wide streets and through the narrow ones, under the archways into the market gardens, across the bridge and into the square where the "glockenspiel" played its old tinkling tune, everywhere the Citadel looked down and always The Rat walked on in his dream. —Frances Hodgson Burnett, *The Lost Prince*, 1914

The music for harp, vibraphone, xylophone, bell-like glockenspiel and cimbalom often possesses the textural delicacy and sound color associated with the music of Mr. Boulez since the premiere in 1955 of "Le Marteau sans Maitre" ("The Hammer Without a Master"), which brought him to public attention. —Barbara Jepson, "Both Challenging and Cool," *The Wall Street Journal*, September 5, 2009

Glockenspiel comes from the German word *glocken*, "bells," which is probably imitative, and *spiel*, "play."

gobbledygook
/(gäb'əl dē gook, *or* gäb'əl dē goōk)/

noun

1 Nonsense; meaningless or encrypted language.
2 Something written in an overly complex, incoherent, or incomprehensible manner.

Examples:
As for Aciman's view of *In the Shadow of Young Girls in Flower*, while I take (and at the time took) the point about heavy-handed literalness, to describe it as "gobbledygook" simply betrays a failure to understand the English language. —Christopher Prendergast, "'Proust's Way?': An Exchange," *The New York Review of Books*, December 15, 2005

One judge told the government its courtroom arguments were "gobbledygook" and invited its lawyer to return to his office and "have a big chuckle." —"Court Skeptical of Wiretap Rules," *Wired*, May 5, 2006

New Class gobbledygook, which is more prevalent than ever, is also more destructive than ever because the government itself is doing more than ever. —"What's Elevated, Health-Care Provider?" *The Wall Street Journal*, May 15, 2009

Rebounding bank profits, a direct result of government giveaways, and gobbledygook from the industry have successfully fogged the issue. —Anna Bernasek, "5 Facts the Finance Industry Would Rather Ignore," *The Huffington Post*, December 10, 2009

This legislation, while cloaked in obscure language and replete with bureaucratic gobbledygook, is a dire threat to our freedom. —Dick Morris, "The Next Battle: Stop Socialism," *The Baltimore Reporter*, January 20, 2010

Gobbledygook is onomatopoeic, or imitative, of the sounds of a turkey.

54

higgledy-piggledy
/ (hig̠ˌəl-dē-pig'əl-dē)/

adjective

1 In confusion; in a disorderly manner; topsy-turvy.
2 Confused; tumbled; disorderly.

noun

• Confusion; disorder.

Examples:

What struck me was the disorder everywhere; books all over the round table; books on the chairs; books on the floor and **higgledy-piggledy**, here a pair of socks, there a hat and cane, and on the floor his overcoat. —Frank Harris, *Oscar Wilde, His Life and Confessions*, 1918

What had been when he arrived a soggy, messy plain strewn with shanties, ragged sidewalks, a **higgledy-piggledy** business heart, was now truly an astounding metropolis which had passed the million mark in population and which stretched proud and strong over the greater part of Cook County. —Theodore Dreiser, *The Titan*, 1914

The Post Road can be seen as a rough American equivalent of the Great Wall of China, i.e., not a carefully planned and constructed creation but one put together **higgledy-piggledy**, with pieces here and there that sometimes connected and sometimes did not. —Jonathan Yardley, "Review: Eric Jaffe's 'The King's Best Highway,'" *The Washington Post*, July 25, 2010

Higgledy-piggledly may be a reduplication—"the repeating of a word or section of a word in order to form a new word or phrase, possibly with modification of one of the repetitions"—of the word *pig* and the image of disorderliness the animal evokes.

(55) **hoi-polloi**
/(hoi̯ pə-loi')/

noun
• The common people; the masses.

Examples:
We hoi-polloi waited for the first-class passengers to finish boarding before crowding onto the plane after them. —Wordnik

And hoi-polloi refers to common people, not those rich morons that are evicting those two red-tail hawks . . . from that 5th Avenue co-ops. —"'Political Jab'; Closing Arguments Set for This Morning in Penalty Phase of Scott Peterson's Trial," CNN Transcripts, December 9, 2004

"He was a VIP prisoner and I was just hoi-polloi," says Ndungane. —"Healing a Priority for New Archbishop," *ANC*, June 5, 1996

Only then did our Cotswold hoi-polloi learn of Master's other proclivities, right down to his string of mistresses (all titled, naturally). —Frank Keating, "Badminton is Still Sparkling After 60 Years," *The Guardian*, May 5, 2009

Hoi-polloi is made up of two Greek words: *hoi*, meaning "the," and *polloi*, meaning "many." Placing "the" in front of *hoi-polloi* is not necessary and is often considered incorrect.

56

honorificabilitudinitatibus

/(ôn'ə rif ik ə bil̯ē tōō di ni tät ə bəs)/

noun
• The state of being able to achieve honors.

Examples:
I marvel thy master hath not eaten thee for a word; for thou art not so long by the head as honorificabilitudinitatibus: thou art easier swallowed than a flap-dragon. —William Shakespeare, *Love's Labour's Lost*, 1598

Like John o'Gaunt his name is dear to him, as dear as the coat and crest he toadied for, on a bend sable a spear or steeled argent, honorificabilitudinitatibus, dearer than his glory of greatest shakescene in the country. —James Joyce, *Ulysses*, 1922

This explanation of the real meaning to be derived from the long word honorificabilitudinitatibus seems to be so convincing as scarcely to require further proof. —Sir Edwin Durning-Lawrence, *Bacon is Shakespeare*

Cos'tard [is] a clown who apes the court wits of Queen Elizabeth's time. He uses the word "**honorificabilitudinitatibus**," and some of his blunders are very ridiculous, as "ad dunghill, at the fingers' ends, as they say . . ." —Selmar Hess, *Character Sketches of Romance, Fiction and the Drama*, 1892

Honorificabilitudinitatibus is an extension of an extension of an extension—a plural form of the Latin, *honorificabilitudinitas*, an extension of *honorificabilitudo*, "honourableness," which itself is an extension of *honorofisabilis*, "honourable."

hooey
/(hōō'ē)/

noun
• Silly talk or writing; nonsense.

Examples:
Two former top aides of President George W. Bush dismiss claims that Vice President Dick Cheney was the "power behind the throne" or the puppetmaster who controlled the Presidency, saying the claims are "myth" or just plain "hooey." —"Former Aides: Cheney Did Not Pull Bush's Strings," *Capitol Hill Blue*, January 2, 2009

But, for the moment, my sense of guilt has subsided and will only resurface many years from now when I frolic in the fields of scorched earth, recounting the days of endless oil consumption, Godless homos trying to marry, and Global Warming "hooey" to my black lunged grandkids and their three headed, glowing dog, Terry Schiavo. —Corinne Marshall, "I Am Destroying the Earth," *The Huffington Post*, June 14, 2009

Hooey may be related to *phooey*, "an expression of disgust, rejection, or disappointment," which probably comes from the Yiddish *pfui*.

58   hurdy-gurdy
/ (hûr͵dē-gûr'dē *or* hûr'dē-gûr͵dē)/

noun

1 A medieval stringed instrument which has a droning sound. One hand turns a handle connected to a wheel which vibrates the strings, while the other hand plays a keyboard to alter the pitch.
2 A barrel organ.

Examples:

Their lodgings are filthy and their food is disgusting, unlike what they ever have at home; they sleep to the harsh strains of a wretched steam hurdy-gurdy which plays day and night in the restaurant under their lodging. —Anton Chekhov, *The Schoolmistress and Other Stories*, 1921

The tech turns the crank like a hurdy-gurdy, and the scooper arms converge on the bottom right corner of the ice sheet and dig in, spraying snow around the room. —Ben Paynter, "Mr. Freeze: How Julian Bayley Turns Ice Cubes Into Ice Castles," *Wired*, December 22, 2008

Like Mr. Froom, they let Mr. Thompson sneak in a hurdy-gurdy or two in the mix, but they didn't allow the purity of the bass-drums-guitar sound to get too cluttered with odds and ends and krumhorns. —David Bowman, "Got Guitar? Richard Thompson Shoots Out the Lights Again," *The New York Observer*, September 19, 1999

Hurdy-gurdy is perhaps onomatopoeic, or imitative, of the sounds of the instrument.

inchoate
/ (in-kō'it)/

adjective

1 Recently started but not fully formed yet; just begun; only elementary or immature.

2 Chaotic, disordered, confused; also, incoherent, rambling.

verb

1 To begin or start something.

2 To cause or bring about.

3 To make a start.

Examples:

When inchoate is used in the sense of "confused, disordered, entangled" by even fairly learned colleagues (with, however, usually no Latin and less Greek), there must be some sort of semantic blund that imparts the sense of chaotic and adds it to the meaning "incipient." —*Verbatim: The Language Quarterly*, Vol. VII, No. 3

[Filmmaker Stanley] Kubrick dreamed of villains like this: nerds in fleece, controlling the information, calling their cult a family. It was an image, a kind of inchoate anxiety about the future, rather than anything you could put your finger on. —Vanessa Grigoriadis, "Do You Own Facebook—Or Does Facebook Own You?" *San Francisco Sentinel*, April 8, 2009

In the *Chronicle of Higher Education*, commentator Sasha Abramsky recently denounced Tea Partiers for "representing little more than an inchoate rage against the zeitgeist." —Eric Felton, "Where Is the Outrage?" *The Wall Street Journal*, July 16, 2010

To inchoate a new habit is easy; to maintain it however is difficult. —Wordnik

Inchoate contains the Latin root *cohum*, meaning "strap from yoke to harness."

60   inculcate
/ (in-kul'kāt *or* in'kul kāt,)/

verb

1 To impress by frequent admonitions, or by forcible statement or argument; enforce or stamp upon the mind.

2 To teach by repeated instruction.

Examples:

The sort of morality which the priests inculcate is a very
subtle policy, far finer than the politicians, and the world
is very successfully ruled by them as the policemen. —Henry
David Thoreau, *A Week on the Concord and Merrimack Rivers*, 1849

Those 12 weeks are devoted to exercises designed to inculcate the Corps' emotional values of honor, courage and
commitment. —Jon R. Katzenbach and Zia Khan, "Money Is Not The
Best Motivator," *Forbes*, April 6, 2010

Though he himself did not characterize his views in these
terms, we can mark his ethos by the term "Religious Hu-
manism"; a conception that joined together a religious
orthodoxy with a determination to inculcate in Jews an
allegiance to modern education and culture. —David Shasha,

"Moses Montefiore: The Most Important Jew of the 19th Century," *The Huffington Post*, June 15, 2010

Prosecutors from South Sudan and Tanzania explain to him how they try to get kids in their countries involved by starting "integrity clubs" in high schools to inculcate anticorruption values early. —Bob Davis, "Corruption Fighters Form Close-Knit Club," *The Wall Street Journal*, July 7, 2010

Inculcate comes from the Latin *inculcāre*, which contains the root *calcare*, meaning "to trample." *Calcare* comes from *calx* or *calc*, meaning "heel."

(61) indefatigable

/ (in͵di-fat'i-gə-bəl)/

adjective

• Not defatigable; incapable of being fatigued; not easily exhausted; not yielding to fatigue; unremitting in labor or effort.

Examples:

Indeed, it seems to me, that while Lucretia Mott may be said to be the soul of this movement, and Mrs. Stanton the mind, the "swift, keen intelligence," Miss Anthony, alert, aggressive, and indefatigable, is its nervous energy—its propulsive force. —Elizabeth Cady Stanton, Susan B. Anthony, and Matilda Joslyn Gage, Editors, *History of Woman Suffrage*, 1886

So restless and **indefatigable** is avarice and ambition, when inflamed by a desire of revenge. —Jonathan Swift, *The Prose Works of Jonathan Swift*, 1902

Here and there certain **indefatigable** spirits, clad all in red after the manner of devils and leaping furiously about with torches, were supposed to affright you. —Henry James, *Italian Hours*, 1909

It has been well said that the very reputation of being strong-willed, plucky, and **indefatigable** is of priceless value. —Orison Swett Marden, *Pushing to the Front*, 1911

In his first words to the press on Tuesday from the Florencia airport in Colombia, Moncayo thanked the "**indefatigable**" Senator Cordoba, Colombians for Peace, the Catholic Church, and the International Red Cross. —Kiraz Janick, "Freed FARC Hostage Thanks Efforts of Venezuelan President to Win His Liberation," *Venezuela Analysis*, March 31, 2010

Some synonyms for *indefatigable* include *unwearied, untiring, tireless, unflagging, persevering, assiduous, persistent,* and *sedulous*.

62

interrobang
/(in târ'ə bang)/

noun
- The punctuation mark, ‽ (a combination of ? and !).

Examples:
[The **interrobang**] is used to portray both a question and a feeling of surprise—perhaps even a little disbelief—when someone tells you something shocking. —Moon Byung-joo, "Customer-centric 'Interrobang' Concept Gains Steam," *JoongAng Daily*, July 20, 2010

Frankly, Bachmann has arrived at the place where she has earned the **interrobang**—"?!" —Jason Linkins, "MSNBC Takes Michele Bachmann's 'Youth Re-Education Camp' Seriously," *The Huffington Post*, April 7, 2009

The **interrobang** is one of my favorite punctuation marks, intended to combine the exclamation mark and the question mark. —Arve Bersvendsen, *Virtuelvis*, September 2009

The **interrobang** was in vogue for much of the 1960s, with the word "interrobang" appearing in some dictionaries and the mark itself being featured in magazine and newspaper articles. —Stephen Coles, "National Punctuation Day Reignites Interrobang Passion," *The FontFeed*, September 24, 2008

It needs to be, ideally, a wacky love comedy featuring non-standard relationships, set at a school, with a huge dose of weirdness. In other words, *Negima!?* (gotta love the **interrobang**). —"Maria Holic—Pander Spectacular or/and Something Mo(r)e?" *Drastic My Anime Blog*, April 19, 2009

Interrobang is a blend of the Latin word *interrogare*, "to ask," and *bang*, printers' slang for the exclamation point.

63 **isthmus**
/(is'məs)/

noun
- A narrow strip of land bordered by water and connecting two larger bodies of land, as two continents, a continent and a peninsula, or two parts of an island.

Examples:
Once the equivalent of a modern multilane highway, the Panama Canal may be on the verge of becoming something closer to an old, congested country road. The increasing number of ships hovering offshore awaiting a chance to cross the **isthmus** is just one sign of the 92-year-old canal's status as a bottleneck. —Amanda Lang, "The Panama Canal at a Crossroads," *OpEdNews.com*, September 4, 2006

The whole isthmus is very rugged, though not high, being a succession of little abrupt hills anal valleys, with angular masses of limestone rock everywhere projecting, and often almost blocking up the pathway. —Alfred Russel Wallace, *The Malay Archipelago*, 1869

An isthmus is a piece of land which saves another piece of land from being an island. —"Teaching Tommy," *Punch, or the London Charivari*, January 29, 1919

A small *isthmus* is often referred to as a *neck*.

64   kinnikinnick
/(ki͵ni ki nik')/

noun
- A mixture of dried leaves, bark, and sometimes tobacco, formerly smoked by some Native Americans.

Examples:
The red willow bark is known as kinnikinnick, and adds a pleasant fragrance to smoking tobacco in the aboriginal estimation. —Henry Wadsworth Longfellow, "Hiawatha; a Poem," 1856

The Indians filled their pipes with kinnikinnick, or willow bark, and smoked. —Edward Eggleston, *Stories of American Life and Adventure*, 1895

Clover gathered a great mat of green scarlet-berried vine like glorified cranberry, which Dr. Hope told her was the famous kinnikinnick, and was just remarking on the cool water-sounds which filled the place, when all of a sudden these sounds seemed to grow angry, the defile of precipices turned a frowning blue, and looking up they saw a great thunder-cloud gathering overhead. —Susan Coolidge, *Clover*, 1907

Making him two elk-horn picks, and filling his ikta with dried salmon and kinnikinnick, he climbed in two nights and a day to the summit. —John H. Williams, *Mountain That was God*, 1911

Popular items include Douglas firs, Western red cedars, sword ferns and kinnikinnick, a low-growing shrub that can fend off weeds by covering broad sections of a lawn. —Andy Rathbun, "Bargains on Native Landscaping at Plant Sale by Snohomish Conservation District," *HeraldNet*, January 18, 2010

Kinnikinnick originated with the Unami tribe in Virginia and North Carolina.

Knickerbocker

65

/ (nik'ər-bok͵ər)/

noun

1 A descendant of the Dutch settlers of New Netherlands.

2 (as *knickerbocker*) A stout fabric of wool and linen having a rough or knotted surface, used for women's dresses.

3 (as *knickerbockers*) Loosely fitting knee-breeches resembling those represented as worn by the Dutch in the seventeenth century.

Examples:

The very word **Knickerbocker** is one evidence of the vitality of Irving's happy imaginings. —Bliss Perry, *The American Spirit in Literature*, 1921

The small boy from the First Reader, legs apart, hands in **knickerbocker** pockets, gazed at the crowd of irresolute elders with scornful wonder. —George Madden Martin, "A Little Feminine Casabianca," *The Speaker*, December 1906

She was in **knickerbocker** costume, had tipped back her chair, one foot on the hearth and the other foot propped on her knee, and she asked Latisan to sit down, pointing to a chair beside her. —Holman Day, *Joan of Arc of the North Woods*, 1922

Knickerbocker comes from the fictitious author Diedrich Knickerbocker of the book *History of New York* (really written by Washington Irving). The New York Knicks, a National Basketball Association team, are actually the New York *Knickerbockers*.

66

lollygag
/ (lol'ē-gag,)/

verb
• To dawdle; to be lazy or idle; to avoid necessary work or effort.

noun
• Silliness, nonsense.

Examples:

I remind myself that I can take as long as I want; it's OK to lollygag looking at all the different kinds of paprika or salami. —W. Hunter Roberts, "Notes of a Temporary Ex-Pat #2 (Week One)," *The Huffington Post*, April 7, 2010

You're an early to bed, early to riser—21 going on 85, you're the kind of person who has to lollygag in the morning when picking out your argyle socks and wool sweater so that you can be sure Collis will be open by the time you get there. —Katy Briggs, "What Type of Sleeper Are You?" *The Dartmouth*, February 26, 2010

The sun warmed up the lookout's wall at our backs and we enjoyed a delightful lollygag while we ate lunch and soaked in the views. —Richard O'Neill, "Wildlife Encounters Leave Mark on Hikes," *The News-Review*, April 4, 2010

According to a new study, of all the hyper-driven personalities reporting on network nightly news, Mr. Tapper is quantitatively the least likely to lollygag. —Felix Gillette, "Tapper on Top! TV's Most Prolific Once Dated 'That Woman'," *The New York Observer*, January 16, 2008

Synonyms for *lollygag* include *dawdle, idle, laze, procrastinate, saunter, trifle, diddle, delay, shirk, slack,* and *loaf.*

lozenge
/(loz'inj)/

noun

1 A plane figure with four equal sides, having two acute and two obtuse angles, also called a *diamond*; a rhomb; also, formerly, any oblique parallelogram.
2 A small cake of sugar, or confection, often medicated, originally in the form of a rhomb, but now variously shaped.
3 A pane of glass for window-glazing, either *lozenge*-shaped or square, but intended to be set diagonally; a quarrel.

4 In *decorative art*, divided by diagonal lines into diamonds or *lozenges*.

Examples:
The beauty of these cakes will depend on the way they are cut. You may choose to make them tablets an inch wide and three inches long, or in lozenge shape—the true diamond—but in either case the cutting must be exact. —Catherine Owen, *Choice Cookery*, 1889

The first idea of window-tracery was the introduction of a plain lozenge-shaped opening over a double lancet window, the whole being covered by a single dripstone. —P. H. Ditchfield, *English Villages*, 1901

If a peppermint lozenge is taken into the mouth, it strongly excites the general sensibilities of taste, and the power of distinguishing between special flavors is lost for a few moments. —Ray Vaughn Pierce, *The People's Common Sense Medical Adviser in Plain English*, 1895

Lozenge comes from the Old French word *losenge,* meaning "windowpane, small square cake."

68 malarkey
/(mə lär'kē)/

noun
* Nonsense; rubbish. Also spelled *malarky*.

Examples:
It's "**malarkey**" that Skilled Healthcare could find the wording confusing, Michael Thamer, an attorney for one of the three firms representing the plaintiffs, told the jury.
—Michael Fumento, "California Trial Lawyers Find a Geezer Goldmine," *Forbes*, July 28, 2010

Griffin wouldn't have dared to make that comment in front of Mark Roberts, or any other knowledgeable de-bunker of his **malarkey**, which is why he's never accepted an invitation to appear with him publicly. —Rob Kall, "Interview with David Ray Griffin on the Rob Kall Radio Show," *OpEdNews.com*, September 22, 2008

If we had capital punishment in accordance with the wishes of the majority of the people, then all this **malarkey** could have been avoided. —Alex Massie, "Lockerbie Decision: The Backlash Begins," *The Spectator*, August 20, 2009

Malarkey may be Irish in origin.

69 molybdenum
/ (mə-lib'də-nəm)/

noun
- A metallic chemical element (symbol Mo) with an atomic number of 42.

Examples:

Molybdenum is a needed element in plants and animals. In plants, for example, the presence of **molybdenum** in certain enzymes allows the plant to absorb nitrogen. Soil that has no **molybdenum** at all cannot support plant life. —"Molybdenum," *The Encyclopedia of Earth*, January 19, 2008

The main use of **molybdenum** is in the manufacture of high-speed tool steels, in which it has been used as a partial or complete substitute for tungsten. —C. K. Leith, *The Economic Aspect of Geology*, 1921

Iron and copper ores frequently contain **molybdenum**, sometimes in quantity; consequently it is met with in slags and pig-iron. —Cornelius Beringer, *A Text-book of Assaying: For the Use of Those Connected with Mines*, 1904

Molybdenum comes from the Greek word molubdos, "lead."

70 mullock
/(mulˈək)/

noun

1 Rubbish; refuse; dirt; dung.

2 In *mining*, rubbish; mining refuse; that which remains after the ore has been separated.

3 A blundered piece of business; a mull or mess.

4 The stump of a tree.

verb

• To work on in a blundering, untidy, or unsatisfactory way; half do (a thing); spoil; botch.

Examples:

The men are hard at work on these hills of "**mullock**," plying the windlasses by which the stuff is brought up from below, or puddling and washing off "the dirt." —Samuel Smiles, *A Boy's Voyage Round the World*, 1905

But the one tiny bit of shiny stuff in the **mullock** heap for Labor is the finding that voters are no better disposed towards Abbott than they are towards Rudd. —Shaun Carney, "Rudd's Risk Factor," *The Sydney Morning Herald*, June 12, 2010

No one wanted Charles as a lab partner as he'd most likely **mullock** everything up. —Wordnik

Mullock was formed by combining *mull*, "dust; rubbish; dirt," and the suffix *-ock*, used to form diminutives.

71

mumbo-jumbo
/(mum'bō jum'bō)/

noun

1 A deity or other supernatural being said to have been worshipped by certain West African peoples; an idol.

2 Any object of superstition; religious words and/or actions which are seen as superstitious or fraudulent.

3 Any confusing or meaningless speech; nonsense, gibberish.

Examples:

Judge Sweet smartly saw through the technical **mumbo-jumbo** that some lawyers have used to defend patents on raw genes. —Matthew Herper, "How Gene Patents Harm Innovation," *Forbes*, April 1, 2010

It will take someone much more intelligent than I to come up with the legal **mumbo-jumbo** to get this thing fixed correctly. —Rob Rang, "NFL Must Follow NCAA's Lead, Add Bite to Bark," *The Washington Post*, August 3, 2010

Tristram Hunt's admiring biography of Engels, "Marx's General," goes further to redress the balance, arguing on behalf of Engels's intellectual contribution and, along the way, showing him to be a more interesting and paradoxical character than the man who pioneered the **mumbo-jumbo** of dialectical materialism. —Rupert Darwall, "The Champagne Communist," *The Wall Street Journal*, August 29, 2009

Used to obsequious **mumbo-jumbo** from the Japanese political class, these critics apparently found it hard to swallow the straight talk about America's shortcomings as an economic model or about the relative decline of American power noted in the essay. —Nathan Gardels, "Lost in Syndication: The Case of the Hatoyama Essay," *The Huffington Post*, September 10, 2009

Mumbo-jumbo may be Mandingo, or West African, in origin.

72

mundungus

/(mən dung'əs)/

noun

- Foul-smelling tobacco. Also, a type of cheap tobacco from Spain.

Examples:

So saying, she sat down to her wheel, and seized, while she spun, her jet-black cutty pipe, from which she soon sent such clouds of vile **mundungus** vapour as must have cleared the premises of Lady Penelope, had she not been strong in purpose to share the expected confession of the invalid. —Sir Walter Scott, *Saint Ronan's Well*, 1823

At a dinner which was given at Trinity College, Cambridge, to the Duke of Gloucester, as Chancellor of the University, when the cloth was removed, Parr at once started his pipe and began, says one who was present, "blowing a cloud into the faces of his neighbours, much to their annoyance, and causing royalty to sneeze by the stimulating stench of **mundungus**." —George Latimer Apperson, *The Social History of Smoking*, 1914

It did not indeed in the least resemble tea, either in smell or taste, or in any particular, unless in being a leaf; for it was in truth no other than a tobacco of the **mundungus** species. —Henry Fielding, *A Journal of a Voyage to Lisbon*, 1755

The boatman tied the skiff to the pier and silently gestured for us to disembark, before going back to his pipe full of stinking **mundungus**. —Wordnik

Mundungus comes from the Spanish word *mondongo*, "tripe, entrails."

73

obstreperous

/ (ob-strep'ər-əs, əb-)/

adjective

1 Attended by, or making, a loud and tumultuous noise; boisterous.

2 Noisily and stubbornly defiant.

Examples:

Is it out of charity for the weakness of human nature and that we may think as well as possible of it—is that why we admire and praise most enthusiastically the kind of love and the kind of friendship and the kind of grief that manifest themselves in obstreperous feeling and wordiness, with no strength left for any attempt to *do*? —David Graham Phillips, *Susan Lenox: Her Fall and Rise*, 1917

"But when I took them back," continued Hetty—and here the tears became again obstreperous and difficult to restrain—"the master said he'd forgot to tell me that this order was for the colonies, that he had taken it at a very low price, and that he could only give me three shillin's for the job." —R. M. Ballantyne, *Dusty Diamonds Cut and Polished*, 1884

The teacher and her "obstreperous" pupils had disappeared from Horsford and had been almost forgotten. —Albion Winegar Tourgée, *Bricks Without Straw: A Novel*, 1880

Synonyms for *obstreperous* include *tumultuous, boisterous, uproarious, clamorous, noisy, unruly,* and *vociferous.*

74 palisade
/ (pal͵i-sād')/

noun

1 A fence made of strong pales or stakes set firmly in the ground, forming an enclosure, or used as a defense.

2 A stake, of which two or more were in former times carried by dragoons, intended to be planted in the ground for defense.

3 A wire sustaining the hair: a feature of the head-dress at the close of the seventeenth century.

verb

• To surround, enclose, or fortify with a palisade or palisades.

Examples:

He showed above the palisade from the waist up, and the morning sunshine touched his cocked hat and buff and blue with an added glory. —Joseph A. Altsheler, *The Riflemen of the Ohio,* 1910

He again beheld the house at Neuilly, where he had been born and where he still lived, that home of peace and toil, with its garden planted with a few fine trees, and parted by a quickset hedge and **palisade** from the garden of the neighbouring house, which was similar to his own. —Émile Zola, *The Three Cities Trilogy*, 1897

Steve's plan was to **palisade** his mansion so that no one could get in and no one could get out. —Wordnik

Palisade is from the French word *palissade*, "stake," and is also called a *swine-feather* and *Swedish feather*.

parsimonious
/ (pär¸sə-mō'nē-əs)/

adjective
• Characterized by parsimony in practice or disposition; very sparing in expenditure; frugal to excess; stinting.

Examples:
The next day, however, Archibald, who was expert in **parsimonious** expedients, considered that he had better delay giving the hostler his half-guinea, till it had been earned by his care of Sawney. —Maria Edgeworth, *Tales and Novels*, 1857

Once that came out, people should have backed off, and maybe Mr. Howard the next time around would use the word "**parsimonious**" instead of "niggardly," knowing that there might be someone close by who might get the wrong impression of the word he was using. —Randall Kennedy, "Nigger: The Strange Career of a Troublesome Word," *Booknotes*, March 3, 2002

When Angela Merkel talks about budget cuts these days she likes to invoke the "Swabian housewife"—Germany's equivalent of the **parsimonious** Scot. —Toby Helm, Ian Traynor, and Paul Harris, "Europe Embraces the Cult of Austerity—but at What Cost?" *The Guardian*, June 13, 2010

Pill-splitting is catching on among **parsimonious** prescription-takers who want to lower costs. —David Whelan, "Saving Big Bucks on Prescription Drugs," *Forbes*, March 4, 2010

Synonyms for *parsimonious* include *avaricious, close, covetous, frugal, mean, miserly, stingy,* and *thrifty.*

76 **passacaglia**
/ (pä‚sə-käl'yə *or* pas‚ə-kal'yə)/

noun

1 An old dance of Italian or Spanish origin, resembling the chaconne.
2 Music for such a dance, or in its rhythm, which is triple and slow.

Examples:

Upon this as cantus firmus Brahms has developed what is known as a **passacaglia**; originally a rather slow and stately dance, but in musical use denoting a movement developed over a ground bass, or single harmonic foundation, the final result partaking somewhat of the nature of variations; but more of a sort of cumulative playing with musical elements, finally reaching a great degree of complexity, which, if well done, should also be a complexity of idea and a fullness and richness of expression. —W. S. B. Mathews, *The Masters and their Music*, 1898

The familiar Welsh lullaby "All Through the Night" is the theme that underlies each movement: the first, a theme and variations, each one in a different key, the second a chaconne and then a **passacaglia** and, finally another set of variations. —Anne Midgette, "In Performance: Emerson Quartet," *The Washington Post*, April 27, 2010

The music proceeds as a kind of parody in **passacaglia**, the same materials given over to shifting textures and rising scales and then more fluid affects. —Gary Lemco, "Reissue CD Reviews," *Audiophile Audition*, February 28, 2009

Passacaglia is from the Spanish word *pascalle*, which is made up of *pasar*, "to pass, step" and *calle*, "street."

77

persnickety
/ (pər-snik'i-tē)/

adjective

1 Fastidious or fussy.

2 Obsessive about mundane details, demanding precision.

Examples:

Ms. Jones says "persnickety" details in recipes, such as asking for a specific size onion, mandating "fussy" ways of cutting vegetables and listing expensive or hard-to-find ingredients, are frustrating home cooks. —Pervaiz Shallwani, "A Shift to Recipe-less Cooking," *The Wall Street Journal*, April 1, 2009

They've been summoned because one of the inmates ("patients," the persnickety head doctor keeps saying, correcting references to them as prisoners) seems to have escaped. —Marshall Fine, "Movie Review: *Shutter Island*," *The Huffington Post*, February 15, 2010

Supreme Court nominee Elena Kagan endured a rather persnickety line of questioning from Sen. Jeff Sessions (R—Ala.) on the ban on military recruiting at Harvard when she was the dean of the law school. —Jonathan Capeheart, "Kagan is Right on 'Don't Ask Don't Tell,'" *The Washington Post*, June 29, 2010

As noted philosopher Dionne Warwick once said, a house is not a home. Now a growing legion of **persnickety** chefs want diners to know that their restaurants aren't either.
—"House Sweet House," *Newsweek*, May 22, 2009

Persnickety, which is used more often in the United States, is an alteration of *pernickety*, which has the same meaning and is used in the United Kingdom.

78 phantasmagoria

/ (fan-taz͵mə-gôr′ē-ə *or* fan-taz͵mə-gōr′ ē-ə)/

noun

1 A fantastic series or medley of illusive or terrifying figures or images.

2 An exhibition of images or pictures by the agency of light and shadow, as by the magic lantern or the stereopticon; especially, such an exhibition so arranged by a combination of two lanterns or lenses that every view dissolves or merges gradually into the next.

3 The apparatus by means of which such an exhibition is produced; a magic lantern or a stereopticon.

Examples:
The effort to crystallize into a creed one's articles of faith in these mental **phantasmagoria** is like carving a cathedral from sunset clouds, or creating salient and retreating lines

of armed hosts in the northern lights. —"Presence," *The Atlantic Monthly*, July 1862

Gilliam's vision is indeed amazing, taking the dreamy psychedelic **phantasmagoria** of his earlier classics, *Brazil* and *Fear and Loathing in Las Vegas*, to a new level in modern day London juxtaposed with the antique carnival world of Doctor Parnassus (Christopher Plummer), in a father-daughter story, and a Faustian bargain with Mr. Nick (Tom Waits). —Regina Weinreich, "The Imaginarium of Doctor Parnassus: Let Them Eat Cake," *The Huffington Post*, December 24, 2009

Phantasmagoria is an alteration of the obsolete French word *phantasmagorie*, "art of creating supernatural illusions," which may be made up of *fantasme*, "illusion," and *allégorie*, "allegory."

79 **piffle**
/ (pif'əl)/

verb
1 To do something (or nothing) in a lazy, ineffective way; idle; dawdle; talk idly or nonsensically.
2 To be squeamish.

noun
• Something trifling or nonsensical; trifling talk; twaddle.

Examples:

"Did I hire you to work," Mr. Grant asked the group loitering in the hall with their coffees, "or to **piffle** about all day?" —Wordnik

It's a stompy, hand-clappy, sloppily enunciated Kyliefication of R&B whose core levels of **piffle** ("It's the truth/It's a fact/I was gone/Now I'm back") are magically transcended by the combined forces of stereo panning and chutzpah. —Kitty Empire, "Kylie: Aphrodite," *The Guardian*, July 4, 2010

Rather reluctantly she played him a few odd bits of her recent work—the outcome of dull, depressing days. . . . "Well, I never heard more maudlin **piffle** in my life!" was his frank comment when she had finished. "If you can't do better than that, you'd better shut the piano and go digging potatoes." —Margaret Pedler, *The Moon Out of Reach*, 1921

While the exact origin of *piffle* is unknown, it may be a blend of *piddle*, "to deal in trifles," and *trifle*, "anything insignificant."

80

pish

/(pish)/

noun

- An exclamation of contempt.

verb
- To express contempt by or as by the exclamation "*Pish!*"

Examples:
He added that Molly had also written to Jack, but to what effect he knew not; only that Jack, after reading it in his presence, had "pish'd" and pocketed it in a huff. —Sir Arthur Thomas Quiller-Couch, *Hetty Wesley*, 1903

My father pished and pshawed when he caught me "poking over" books, but my dear mother was inclined to regard me as a genius, whose learning might bring renown of a new kind into the family. —Juliana Horatia Gatty Ewing, *We and the World*, 1881

And when my lady hinted to my lord that he played more than she liked, he dismissed her with a "pish," and swore that nothing was more equal than play betwixt gentlemen, if they did but keep it up long enough. —William Makepeace Thackeray, *The History of Henry Esmond, Esq.*, 1852

The gipsy finding he was not displeased in his heart, told him, after a further inquiry into his hand, that his true-love was constant, and that she should dream of him to-night: my old friend cried "pish," and bid her go on. —Joseph Addison, Eustace Budgell, and Sir Richard Steele, *The De Coverley Papers*, 1920

In the same context as *pish*, one might also say *posh*, *pshaw*, *tush*, and *phooey*.

81 **plesiosaurus**
/(plē'sē ə sôr͵əs)/

noun

- A genus of *Reptilia*, typical of the order *Plesiosauria*, and formerly conterminous with it, now restricted to forms from the Upper Triassic (Rhætic) and the Liassic, as *P. dolichodirus*, with an extremely long neck.

Examples:

Already in 1823 other gigantic creatures, christened ichthyosaurus and plesiosaurus by Conybeare, had been found in deeper strata of British rocks; and these, as well as other monsters whose remains were unearthed in various parts of the world, bore such strange forms that even the most sceptical could scarcely hope to find their counterparts among living creatures. —Henry Smith Williams, *A History of Science*, 1904

Mainstream biology today holds the same position it did in June, 1972, when Rines first saw "a large, darkish hump, covered . . . with rough, mottled skin, like the back of an elephant": there is no plesiosaurus, nor any other aquatic dinosaur, nor slithering monstrosity of any kind, in the murky depths of Loch Ness. —Ben H. Winters, "Robert Rines: The Death of a Monster Hunter," *The Huffington Post*, November 11, 2009

Amy had once said that if Jessie went to her mother and asked if she could have a pet **plesiosaurus**, Mrs. Norwood would say: "Of course, you may, dear. But don't bring it into the house when its feet are wet." —Margaret Penrose, *The Campfire Girls of Roselawn*, 1900s

Plesiosaurus comes from the Greek words *plesios*, "near," and *sauros*, "lizard."

82

polydactyly
/(pä li dak'tə lē)/

noun
- The condition of having many digits—that is, more than the normal number of fingers or toes; the state of being polydactyl.

Examples:

The boy's condition, **polydactyly**, is a relatively rare genetic disorder. Usually with this condition, the extra digits are on the little finger side of the hand. The Chinese boy seems to have central **polydactyly**, a rarer disorder in which the middle fingers are affected, according to the Daily Mail. —Rosemary Black, "Six-year-old Chinese Boy with 31

Fingers and Toes Has Extra Digits Removed Through Surgery," *New York Daily News*, March 24, 2010

It is shortsightedness not to see past one's own privileged race and gender, blinding oneself from recognizing the source of human conflict since time memorial: hierarchical privilege based on race, gender, religion, bloodline, polydactyly, or some other construct. —Rady Ananda, "Sex, Race and War," *OpEdNews.com*, April 14, 2008

Sticking together meant a higher chance of inheriting a disease. The Amish, for example, are more likely to carry a genetic mutation for a condition called polydactyly, which causes extra fingers or toes. —Claudia Kalb, "In Our Blood," *Newsweek*, February 6, 2006

Polydactyly comes from the Greek word *polydaktylos*, meaning "many fingers."

(83)   **poppycock**
/ (pop'ē-kok͵)/

noun
• Trivial talk; nonsense; stuff and rubbish.

Examples:

Peter Briggs hoped he would dare to call it "poppycock" in the presence of his master—for he was thoroughly sick of being a sleuth in the ill-smelling Eleventh Ward. —Holman Day, *The Landloper: The Romance of a Man on Foot*, 1915

In the wake of the Twinkie defense, a representative of the ITT-owned Continental Baking Company asserted that the notion that overdosing on the cream-filled goodies could lead to murderous behavior was "poppycock" and "crap"—apparently two of the artificial ingredients in Twinkies, along with sodium pyrophosphate and yellow dye—while another spokesperson for ITT couldn't believe "that a rational jury paid serious attention to that issue." —Paul Krassner, "Behind the Infamous Twinkie Defense," *The Huffington Post*, December 4, 2008

Gerry Doherty, leader of the TSSA union, and a vocal opponent of Network Rail's bonus payments, said the company's claims of record punctuality were "poppycock." —Dan Milmo, "Network Rail Talks Up Cost Savings and Punctuality," *The Guardian*, June 3, 2010

David Bowie has described reports he is set to headline this year's Coachella festival in Los Angeles as "poppycock." —Jason Gregory, "David Bowie: 'Coachella Festival Claims Are Poppycock,'" *Gigwise*, January 28, 2009

Poppycock is from the Dutch word *pappekak*, made up of *pappe*, "soft dung," plus *kak*, "dung," which comes from the Latin, *cacāre*, "to defecate."

84 pulchritude
/ (pul'kri-tōōd, *or* pul'kri-tyōōd,)/

noun
• Beauty; comeliness; handsomeness.

Examples:
Not that any lady's **pulchritude** is a handicap to a stage career or in any way undesirable. On the contrary, the stage has always welcomed beautiful women, and will continue to do so. —Ned Wayburn, *The Art of Stage Dancing*, 1925

Shopaholism versus workaholism, skin-deep beauty versus inner drive: every piece of jewelry, every strand of exquisitely groomed hair, every inch of exposed flesh signifies some sort of choice between preserving professional, feminist integrity (we know how long it takes to look like that!) and succumbing to crass youth-and-marketing ideals in **pulchritude**. —Molly Haskell, "Cleavage vs. Crime: Do Law & Order Starlets Pretty Up to Move Up?" *The New York Observer*, June 5, 2005

This time Langdon is followed around the Vatican and Rome by an Israeli actress, Ayelet Zurer, who plays the Italian scientist Vittoria Vetra; she's seldom at a loss, though the production gains little more from her presence than physicist **pulchritude**. —Joe Morgenstern, "Plot's Knots Bedevil 'Angels,'" *The Wall Street Journal*, May 22, 2009

Synonyms for *pulchritude* include *beauty, grace, loveliness, cheesecake* ("imagery of scantily clad, sexually attractive persons, especially young women"), and *beefcake* ("imagery of muscular, wellbuilt men; such a male, especially as seen as physically desirable").

85   quackery
/(kwaˈkə rē)/

noun
- The boastful pretensions or knavish practice of a quack, particularly in medicine; empiricism; charlatanry; humbug.

Examples:
The adventures of Doctor Macaire need not be described, because the different degrees in **quackery** which are taken by that learned physician are all well known in England, where we have the advantage of many higher degrees in the science, which our neighbors know nothing about. — William Makepeace Thackeray, *The Paris Sketch Book*, 1852

[G]erontology—the study of aging and of medicinal tools to block its unwanted effects. . . . [a] field that was once shunned as **quackery** is now inviting billions of dollars in pharmaceutical investment and is, as Mr. Stipp says, going mainstream. —Scott Gottlieb, "Gerontology Comes of Age," *The Wall Street Journal*, July 8, 2010

If there's a group that's better at taking legitimate scientific studies and extrapolating from them far beyond what reason, science, medicine, or ethics would ever allow or even what the scientists doing the research could imagine in their worst nightmares, it's the autism anti-vaccine **quackery** movement. —"The Anti-vaccine 'Biomed' Movement: Hijacking Legitimate Scientific Research," *Science Blogs*, November 24, 2009

Quackery and *quack* come from the obsolete Dutch, *quac*, "unguent," or *quacken*, "to boast."

86

ranunculus
/ (rə-nungˈkyə-ləs)/

noun
• Any plant of the genus Ranunculus; the buttercup or crowfoot.

Examples:

Among early summer flowers in open borders few are prettier than the double-flowered kinds of **ranunculus** of the herbaceous type. —"Double Buttercups," *Scientific American Supplement*, November 11, 1882

Madame Sand walked in her garden daily among her marigolds, snapdragon and **ranunculus**, making curious speculations as to what might be in store for herself and her possessions. —Bertha Thomas, *Famous Women: George Sand*, 1883

As for vegetables, there would not have been a flowering plant in all Genoa, if tulip and **ranunculus** roots had not been bitter as aloes. —Maurice Tiernay, "The Soldier of Fortune," *Harper's New Monthly Magazine*, July 1851

Ranunculus comes from the Latin word *rānunculus*, "a kind of medicinal plant," which is diminutive of *rāna*, "frog." *Rana* may be onomatopoetic in origin, imitating the sound of a frog.

87 **rigmarole**
/ (rĭg'mə-rōl͵) /

noun

- A succession of confused or foolish statements; an incoherent, long-winded harangue; disjointed talk or writing; balderdash; nonsense.

109

adjective

- Consisting of or characterized by *rigmarole*; long-winded and foolish; prolix; hence, formal; tedious.

Examples:

I repeat that the only morsel of truth in all this rigmarole is that the books were sent by Dickens, and acknowledged by Mr. Helps at the Queen's desire. —John Forster, *The Life of Charles Dickens*, 1875

I'm not a conspiracy buff, but the fact that all companies do this makes me wonder if this whole senseless rigmarole is actually an insidious corporate plot against consumers. —John Blumenthal, "Is Customer Service a Corporate Conspiracy?" *OpEdNews.com*, December 28, 2009

The employees assumed the holiday party would be fun and informal; however, when they were asked to memorize an "elevator pitch" as a means of introducing themselves, they knew they were in for a rigmarole. —Wordnik

Rigmarole may be an alteration of *ragman roll*, a long scroll of character descriptions used in Ragman, a medieval game of chance.

88 **satsuma**

/(sat-sōō'mə *or* sä-tsōō'mä *or* sä'tsōō-mä)/

noun

1 A type of tangerine, originally grown in Kyushu, Japan.
2 A type of Japanese porcelain.

Examples:

A **satsuma** is a quintessential part of Christmas (although we don't seem to mind if it's a **satsuma**, clementine or any other orange citrus fruit). —Claire Coleman, "90,000 miles! The Astonishing Distance Your Christmas Dinner Travels to Your Plate," *Daily Mail*, December 21, 2009

Like the names of restaurant dishes here—"Creole cream-cheese cannoli with pistachios and **satsuma** sorbet"—the costumed performance feels like a seduction. —Nancy Dewolf Smith, "New Orleans Done Over, Done Right," *The Wall Street Journal*, April 9, 2010

A visit to one of the **satsuma** factories is an interesting experience, as it shows how little the art of Japan has been influenced by the foreigner. —George Hamlin Fitch, *The Critic in the Orient*, 1913

Bits of carved ivory, rich lacquer ware and choice pieces of **satsuma** and cloisonné appeared in the windows. —Mabel Thayer Gray and Elizabeth Gray Potter, *The Lure of San Francisco*, 1915

There is some very good cloisonne, some kisku, and one or two pieces in awaji-yaki. Also there is some **satsuma**, if you would like it. —Roy Eliot Stokes, *Andy at Yale*, 1914

Satsuma is named for its region of origin, a peninsula of southwest Kyushu, Japan.

89 **schlep**
/ (shlep)/

verb
1 To carry or drag around.
2 To move slowly, or as if burdened.

noun
• A long or tedious journey.

Examples:
Recent pop cultural crossovers include a bumper crop of music video tributes to the candidates online, record ratings for "Saturday Night Live" and its send-up of the news, and comedian Sarah Silverman's call for young Jews to make a "great **schlep**" to Florida and nudge their grandpar-

ents toward the Democratic ticket. —John Jurgensen, "Hitting the Polls, Then the Mall," *The Wall Street Journal*, October 24, 2008

The WPA guides, or as they were known in the 1930s, the American Guides, were designed less to encourage tourism than to serve as histories: The WPA directors recognized that most people weren't willing to schlep around something the size of an unabridged dictionary to every natural spring and beach listed in the exhaustive itineraries. —Rebecca Bengal, "Following the dust tracks: Touring Florida through the eyes of Zora Neale Hurston," *The Washington Post*, April 18, 2010

I'd rather not drill there either, because surveys suggest the haul is not worth the effort, but I'm not going to pretend that I want to throw the family in the car and schlep up to the tundra to chase after the noble caribou. —Jason Linkins, "TV SoundOff: Sunday Talking Heads," *The Huffington Post*, May 2, 2010

Schlep comes from a Yiddish word meaning "drag" or "pull."

90 **scintillating**
/ (sin'tl-āt͵ing)/

adjective
1 That *scintillates* with brief flashes of light.
2 Brilliantly clever, amusing or witty.

verb
- Present participle of *scintillate*.

Examples:

He applied it to the lock; the cover flew backward, and a dazzling light flashed into his face as a ray of sunlight fell across his shoulder upon the superb gems, gleaming and **scintillating** from the depths of their hiding-place. —A. Maynard Barbour, *That Mainwaring Affair*, 1901

Her gorgeous trailing robe of gold-embroidered velvet, her under gown of satin **scintillating** with diamonds, her blazing crown of jewels, the sparkling rings on her delicate fingers, her necklaces, her bracelets, were such as the Mother of Christ never dreamed of in her simple life; and half the watchers knew grinding poverty, which a few of her gems might relieve. —A. M. Williamson and C. N. Williamson, *The Car of Destiny*, 1907

The England centre-forward has been in **scintillating** form this season, notching 19 Premier League goals to lead the way for the Red Devils as they adapt to life without Cristiano Ronaldo. —"Rooney not interested in La Liga," *The Irish Times*, January 26, 2010

Scintillating comes from the Latin word *scintillāre*, "spark." A *scintilla* is "a spark; a glimmer; hence, the least particle; a trace."

91 scuppernong

/ (skup'ər-nông, *or* skup'ər-nong₎)/

noun

- A cultivated variety of the muscadine, bullace, or southern foxgrape, *Vitis rotundifolia* (*V. vulpina*), of the southern United States and Mexico. It is a valued white- or sometimes purple-fruited grape. Its large berries are well flavored, and peculiar in that all on a bunch do not ripen at once. The ripe berries fall from the vine, and are gathered from the ground.

Examples:

The luscious scuppernong holds first rank among our grapes, though we cultivate a great many other varieties, and our income from grapes packed and shipped to the Northern markets is quite considerable. —Charles W. Chesnutt, "The Goophered Grapevine," *Martin Luther King, Jr. Day, 1995, Memorial Issue*

He has succeeded in producing one thousand dyes from vegetable substances, including forty-nine from the scuppernong grape alone. —Raleigh H. Merritt, *From Captivity to Fame or The Life of George Washington Carver*, 1929

I was very ill for several days on the way up, the result of malaria—perhaps too many scuppernong grapes at Pass

Christian, and jolting of the heavy army wagon that makes a small stone seem the size of a boulder. —Frances M. A. Roe, *Army Letters from an Officer's Wife*, 1871–1888

Scuppernong is probably of Native American origin. There is also a Scuppernong River in North Carolina.

92 scuttlebutt
/(skut'l-but,)/

noun
• Gossip, rumor, idle chatter.

Examples:
At the time of his departure, an internal WaPo memo suggested that Hoffman had "decided to move on," but the scuttlebutt is that he did not go as willingly as that memo suggests. —Jason Linkins, "A Critical Look at the WaPo Pulitzers," *The Huffington Post*, April 21, 2010

Suffice it to say that the scuttlebutt is that final rankings would often be determined "at a cocktail party [of the figure-skating association], and nothing short of withdrawal of a couple from competition would ever change that order for that year," says Nancy Nelson, a onetime skater who crusades for judging reform. —Sharon Begley, "Our Sport Has Gangrene," *Newsweek*, February 25, 2002

The logic behind the latest **scuttlebutt** is that Biden would be "too old" to run for president in 2012 (he'd be 70 by the time he took office; Hillary would be 65), and, as we've noted, Hillary's denials about wanting to run for president again are less than airtight. —Dan Amira, "Could Hillary Clinton Replace Joe Biden on the Ticket in 2012?" *New York Magazine*, November 25, 2009

A *scuttlebutt* was originally "a keg of water on board ship, around which sailors would gossip."

93   serendipity
/ (ser͵ən-dip′i-tē)/

noun
- The happy faculty, or luck, of finding, by "accidental sagacity," interesting items of information or unexpected proofs of one's theories; discovery of things unsought.

Examples:
I had the thought to go to the website of Joshua Bell and look up where he performed in New York in 2007—and lo and behold, he played at one of the schools on the list my friend had given me!! That kind of **serendipity** is what I'm always looking for. —Jennie Nash, "The Making of a Novel: What Serendipity Has to Do With It," *The Huffington Post*, July 20, 2010

But Rickey is also the author of a fine piece of advice in this commencement season, that "luck is the residue of design." This idea of planning with an eye on serendipity is one of the least-appreciated skills any leader can possess.
—"Lights, Camera, 'Question Time'!" *Newsweek*, May 17, 2008

In concluding his presentation, Keith noted that public spaces do not appear to constitute a public realm for wireless Internet users, but may offer new opportunities for engagement—with copresent but not co-located others—in the public sphere . . . and while serendipity is nice, it probably is not vital to a public space. —Joe McCarthy, "Communities, Technologies and Participation: Notes from C&T 2009," *Gumption*, July 4, 2009

Serendipity was coined by the English author Horace Walpole, inspired by the Persian fairy tale, *The Three Princes of Serendip*, who made *serendipitous* discoveries.

94 **sesquipedalian**
/ (ses͵kwi-pi-dāl'yən)/

adjective

1 Containing or measuring a foot and a half; often humorously said of long words.
2 Addicted to the use of long words.

Examples:

The world that we live in today is sometimes mistaken for a world abounding in political jargon—**sesquipedalian** phrases and groups and corporations and all other flotsam and jetsam that bob along the sea of confusion. —Arjun Rajkhowa, "America's détente with the Muslim World," *The Wall Street Journal*, June 11, 2009

Buckley was a bon vivant with luxurious tastes, a prolific author of best-selling novels as well as serious nonfiction, a sportsman most gleeful on icy slopes and navigating through a gale, a world-class namedropper, a refined musicologist (and self-taught harpsichord player) and a lover of big words (a **sesquipedalian**, as he might say). —Evan Thomas, "He Knew He Was Right" *Newsweek*, March 1, 2008

He would use the simplest, plainest language, he said to himself over and over again; but it is not always easy to use simple, plain language—by no means so easy as to mount on stilts, and to march along with **sesquipedalian** words, with pathos, spasms, and notes of interjection. —Anthony Trollope, *Framley Parsonage*, 1861

Sesquipedalian is a literal translation of a phrase from the Latin poet Horace, who wrote of *sesquipedalia verba* (words a foot and a half long).

shandygaff

/ (shan'dē-gaf͵)/

noun
• A mixture of bitter ale or beer with ginger-beer.

Examples:
And when he came, heated, tired, but bubbling over with eagerness to tell her of the fun they had been having with Brax, she met him with a cool tankard of "**shandygaff**," which he had learned to like in England among the horse-artillery fellows, and declared the very prince of drinks after active exercise in hot weather. —Charles King, *Waring's Peril*, 1894

There would always be weighty enquiries as to what they could have, and it would work out always at cold beef and pickles, or fried ham and eggs and **shandygaff**, two pints of beer and two bottles of ginger beer foaming in a huge round-bellied jug. —H. G. Wells, *The History of Mr. Polly*, 1910

It is believed that a continual bibbing of **shandygaff** saps the will, the nerves, the resolution, and the finer faculties, but there are those who will abide no other tipple. —Christopher Morley, *Shandygaff*, 1918

The original English recipe for *shandygaff* is to combine a pint of bitter beer with a small bottle of old-fashioned ginger-beer. Occasionally porter or stout or lager-beer is substituted for the bitter beer, and ginger ale for the spicier ginger-beer.

96 skullduggery
/(skəl dəg'ə rē)/

noun
• Activities intended to deceive; a con or hoax.

Examples:
Our zoo of financial **skullduggery** is far more complex, with many more moving pieces, than that of the 1920s.
—Frank Rich, "The Other Plot to Wreck America," *The New York Times*, January 9, 2010

Was this an unintentional screw up by a well-meaning Obama staffer trying to clean up a document so it was easier to see online or evidence of some kind of **skullduggery**?
—Thomas Lipscomb, "Why Running 'On the Record' Is Harder Than You Think," *The Huffington Post*, June 29, 2008

Only, like Mel Brooks' cool children, the brothers regard the spy genre as funny at heart, worthy of ribbing even as serious **skullduggery** is undertaken and the body count slowly mounts. —David Luhrssen, "Burn After Reading," *Express Milwaukee*, September 18, 2008

Skullduggery is probably an alteration of the Scottish word *sculduddery,* "obscenity, fornication."

smithereens

/ (smi*th*ˌə-rēnz')/

noun
* Fragments or splintered pieces; numerous tiny disconnected items.

Examples:

When it comes to actually dealing with an asteroid, the Hollywood option, of nuking it to smithereens, is the least useful, says Mr. Schweickart, largely because you can't control the debris. —Lee Gomes, "Keeping the Earth Asteroid-Free Takes Science, Soft Touch," *The Wall Street Journal*, March 19, 2008

Now, reportedly broke, or broke by the standards of people with great wealth—his yacht gone, his planes gone, his dozen houses gone, or going, and his reputation in smithereens—he has recently spent three months pacing restlessly in a six-by-eight-foot prison cell in Bern, Switzerland, where the majority of his fellow prisoners were in on drug charges. —Dominick Dunne, "Khashoggi's Fall," *Vanity Fair,* September 1989

Then you have a beautiful calm without a cloud, smooth sea, placid, crew and cargo in **smithereens**, Davy Jones' locker, moon looking down so peaceful. —James Joyce, *Ulysses*, 1922

Chairs were flung over with a crash, tables were vaulted with a noise like thunder, screens were smashed, crockery scattered in **smithereens**, and still Basil Grant bounded and bellowed after the Rev. Ellis Shorter. —G. K. Chesterton, *The Club of Queer Trades*, 1905

Smithereens comes from the Irish Gaelic *smidirín*, "small fragment."

snaffle
98 /(snaf'əl)/

noun
• A bridle consisting of a slender bit-mouth with a single rein and without a curb; a *snaffle*-bit.

verb
1 To bridle; hold or manage with a bridle.
2 To clutch or seize by the *snaffle*.
3 To purloin, or obtain by devious means.

123

Examples:

In Ireland, where the large majority of our hunters come from, the snaffle is the bit used in breaking and hunting, as it is in steeple-chasing; and although our Irish neighbours find the curb has its advantages, we must admit that they keep it in its proper place and do not allow it to usurp the snaffle when riding over fences. —Alice M. Hayes, *The Horsewoman*, 1903

He muttered something that a snaffle was the safest bit a sinner could place faith in—assumed the mantle of prophecy—foretold, as it would appear, troublous times to be in rapid advent—and inculcated that faith should be placed in heaven, and powder kept very dry. —W. H. Maxwell, "Frank Hamilton; Or, The Confessions of an Only Son," *International Weekly Miscellany*, July 29, 1850

The enemy, of course, played the same game, and unfortunately on one occasion managed to snaffle the N.C.O. and two men from one of our posts. —Captain W. C. C. Weetman, *The Sherwood Foresters in the Great War*, 1920

A *bradoon* is a type of *snaffle* bit. It has small rings and usually is used on a double bridle in conjunction with a curb bit.

99

snickerdoodle
/ (snik'ər dōōd'l)/

noun
- A cookie where the batter is rolled into a ball and coated with cinnamon sugar.

Examples:

I had the case lined with pies, and people'd come in and they'd get a blueberry muffin and they'd get a carrot cake cupcake and they'd get a snickerdoodle cookie, and I was like, "But there's pie!" —Amanda Abrams, "First Person Singular: Teresa Velazquez, Bakery Owner and Pie Maker," *The Washington Post*, August 1, 2010

It didn't taste all that much like a chocolate chip cookie: "snickerdoodle," "sugar cookie," and "straight-up dough" were a few of the comments. —Carey Jones, "Chocolate Chip Cookie Championship: The Downtown Edition," *Serious Eats: New York*, November 23, 2009

Yeager and Copley are already working on other dough flavors, including snickerdoodle and lemon zest, as well as a boxed version of the product that would include instructions for variations in the recipe that customers can customize to meet their dietary and allergen needs. —Christian Conte,

"Moms Sign Deal with Whole Foods to Provide Gluten-free Cookies," *Jacksonville Business Journal*, February 6, 2009

And on other holidays or any other day of the year, they filled our bellies with their apple pies, **snickerdoodle** cookies, angel biscuits, and hot fried chicken. —Beth Arnold, "A Moveable Feast," *The Huffington Post*, November 27, 2008

In addition to *snickerdoodles*, other kinds of cookies include *macaroons, pinwheels, chocolate chip,* and *biscotti.*

100 · sockdolager
/(sok dôl'ə gər)/

noun
1 A hard hit, a knockout or finishing blow.
2 Something exceptional.

Examples:
A "**sockdolager**" is something that settles a matter, as with a decisive blow; it also means something that is extraordinary. —Brian Mackey, "Theatre Centre Stages Last Play Lincoln Saw," *The State-Journal Register*, February 7, 2009

Because we've had a **sockdolager** of a winter—long, windy, often bitterly cold, perhaps unprecedentedly snowy—most of us are feeling a little cabin feverish. —Clay Jenkinson, "Easter: Among Other Things, the Return of the Light," *The Bismarck Tribune*, April 11, 2009

"Of all the swivel-eyed, up-jumped, cross-grained, sons of a cock-eyed tinker," exclaimed Bill, boiling with rage. "If punching parrots on the beak wasn't too painful for pleasure, I'd land you a sockdolager on the muzzle that 'ud lay you out till Christmas." —Norman Lindsay, *The Magic Pudding*, 1918

Sockdolager originally meant just a strong blow. . . . "That was a sockdolager of a punch you landed on me," or, "That was a sockdolager of a speech." In fact, blizzard, which is from 1825, is a similar word. —Allan Metcalf and David Barnhart, "America In So Many Words," *Booknotes*, January 18, 1998

Sockdolager may have been formed by combining *sock*, "to hit hard," and *doxology*, "an expression of praise to God."

101 **spackle**
/ (spak'əl)/

noun

1 Any powder that when mixed with water forms a plastic paste used to fill cracks and holes in plaster.

2 A plastic paste meant for filling cracks and holes in plaster.

verb
- To fill or repair with a plastic paste or *spackle*.

Examples:
The simplest way is by filling grooves in with a vinyl spackling compound using a small putty knife. More than one application may be required since the spackle is likely to shrink. —James and Morris Carey, "How to Convert Old-fashioned Wood Paneling," *The Chippewa Herald*, March 27, 2009

The former Chrysler chairman and author of the book *Where Have All the Leaders Gone* is one of a series of real-life figures from the past 40 years who show up, played by actors in spackle make-up, to take their lumps for alternative history. —A. S. Hamrah, "Review: *Watchmen*," *The Boston Phoenix*, March 6, 2009

A wondrous land where more than $500 million a year is spent off-budget; a land where $500 million does not appear on a single tax bill; a land where $500 million is spent to spackle the cracks of waste, bloat, patronage, and corruption. —Tom Tresser, "Change Comes to Washington, Will It Come to Chicago?" *The Huffington Post*, January 20, 2009

Spackle was originally a trademark but is now used as a generic word.

(102) spelunking
/(spi ləng' king)/

noun
- The practice or hobby of exploring underground caverns; caving.

Examples:

The current approach to documentary-making seems to be simply: choose a random cuddly TV type who everybody likes, send them to a random location on another continent, and have them do something random like swim with sharks or go spelunking. —Pete Cashmore, "Stephen Tompkinson's Australian Balloon Adventure," *The Guardian*, August 14, 2010

As a result, he believes that the kind of technical person who once would have wound up working for a hedge fund on Wall Street will now work at a firm whose business hinges on making smart, daring choices—decisions based on surprising results gleaned from algorithmic spelunking and executed with the confidence that comes from really doing the math. —Steven Levy, "Secret of Googlenomics: Data-Fueled Recipe Brews Profitability," *Wired*, May 22, 2009

Some of the effort Gevisser devoted to spelunking through the hidden recesses of Thabo Mbeki's psyche might have been more usefully expended on the split personality of the movement that fostered and then spurned him, a governing party with the instincts of a beleaguered underground attuned to fending off the next attack. —Joseph Lelyveld, "How Mbeki Failed," *The New York Review of Books*, April 9, 2009

Spelunking comes from the Greek word *spēlunks*, "cave, cavern, grotto," and can also mean "deep exploration" in a figurative sense.

103 **spondulics**
/(spon dōō' liks *or* spon dyōō' liks)/

noun
• Originally, paper money; now, any money; funds. Also, *spondulicks*.

Examples:
Faith, if I had spondulics like you, I wouldn't amuse myself by trudging that way along the roads at night—'Tisn't safe along here. —Guy de Maupassant, *The Works of Guy de Maupassant*, 1909

"Hand over your spondulics, young feller," said the second gentleman of the road. —Horatio Alger, *Struggling Upward*, 1868

I ain't as rich as old Jim Hornback . . . but I've told him a many a time 't I wouldn't trade places with him; for, says I, a sailor's life's the life for me, and I'm derned if *I'd* live two mile out o' town, where there ain't nothing ever goin' on, not for all his **spondulicks** and as much more on top of it. —Mark Twain, *Adventures of Huckleberry Finn*, 1912

If you are reading this, you've pondered it: how cool would it be to play your favorite sport at your house? Some people accrue enough space & **spondulicks** to do it and put up a tennis court or squash court. —James Zug, "I'll Dream Your Dream For You: One Man's Racquet Playland," *Vanity Fair*, June 17, 2009

Spondulics has several spelling variations, including *spondulicks* and *spondulix*.

104 **sprag**
/(sprag)/

noun
1 A billet of wood.
2 A short wooden prop used to support the coal during the operation of holing or undercutting; a punch-prop.

verb
• To prop by a sprag; also, to stop, as a carriage on a steep grade, by putting a sprag in the spokes of the wheel.

Examples:
A new worker's attempts to "**sprag**," or stop the wheels, the cars with a piece of wood was in vain and the three

loaded cars plummeted down the shaft and crashed into the descending elevator, Wolensky and Hastie said. —Janine Ungvarsky, "Remembering the Exeter Mine Disaster 111 Years Later," *The Times Leader*, November 16, 2009

You can gang back to your tippy wee baggage! Gang to hell, baith you an' her, an' joy be wi' you baith! But I'll put a sprag in your wheel afore you gang far. —James C. Welsh, *The Underworld: The Story of Robert Sinclair, Miner*, 1920

For all that, it's a sheer impossibility that you should guess who put a sprag in the wheel of Hilton's chariot. Give you three tries, for a new hat. —Louis Tracy, *The Strange Case of Mortimer Fenley*, 1919

Sprag may be of Scandinavian origin.

105 **squit**
/(skwit)/

noun
1 A person of low status.
2 Nonsense; amusing stories.

Examples:
He made several overtures, but they were all rejected, the reason being that boys of the second division could not

let a "third division **squit**" into their secret. —Maurice Baring, *Orpheus in Mayfair and Other Stories and Sketches*, 1909

The festival continues this week at venues around the town, from a concert of songs from the shows to an evening of **squit** with Sid Kipper. —Ian Clarke, "Dereham Festival Launched in a Blaze of Sunshine," *EDP 24*, May 24, 2010

But this simple statement, following the Pound's loss of a third of its value on the international money markets, that the British Currency MAY be in a spot of bother seems to have provoked YET MORE opprobrium for the gormless Gideon. Indeed the Labour now accuse HIM of causing the Sterling Crisis (as though the City would pay a blind bit of notice to anything the little **squit** had to say). —"Master Gideon Gaffes Again!" *The Very Fluffy Diary of Millennium Dome, Elephant*, November 18, 2008

Squit may originate from a similar dialect word of Norfolk, England.

106 synecdoche
/(si-nek′də-kē)/

noun
- In *rhetoric*, a figure or trope by which the whole of a thing is put for a part, or a part for the whole, as the genus for the species, or the species for the genus, etc.: as, for example, a fleet of ten *sail* (for *ships*); a master employing new *hands* (for *workmen*).

Examples:

A "synecdoche" is a grammatical term meaning the part for the whole, like referring to headlights to describe a car driving down the road. The title might refer to the constantly mutating theater piece as the physical manifestations of Caden's psychological state. Or the term might refer to Caden, as an alter ego, or kind of synecdoche of Kaufman himself. —Rachel Abramowitz, "The Critical Words? Every One Stings," *Los Angeles Times*, October 26, 2008

But maybe the truth is that every mailperson in the City has knowledge to pass on, because the West 20th Street block between Eighth and Ninth Avenues is no more nor less than a city synecdoche. —David Finkle, "Do You Know the Muffin Man? Yes, He Lives Down the Block," *The Huffington Post*, August 17, 2009

Synecdoche is similar to *metonymy*, "a trope or figure of speech that consists in substituting the name of one thing for that of another to which the former bears a known and close relation," such as *Washington* for the United States government.

107 · synesthesia
/(sin͵əs *thē*'zhə)/

noun

- The production of a sensation located in one place when another place is stimulated, such as seeing specific colors when hearing a particular instrument, etc.

Examples:

Synesthesia is the perception of two unlike sensory modalities at once. For example, some synesthetes report reading or hearing a name and instantly associating it with a color, gender, or taste. —April Pierce, "Synesthesia and Metaphor: Between Fact and Fiction," *The Huffington Post*, August 12, 2010

Mr. Lewis observed that some of Ms. Saariaho's music struck him as a kind of synesthesia: that the sound of her music seemed almost to invoke pictures. —Allan Kozinn, "Finnish Composer Bursts Some of Her Own Myths," *The New York Times*, November 25, 2009

Clearly, synesthesia is related to creativity. A new survey by Grossenbacher found that out of 84 synesthetes, 26 were professional artists, writers or musicians, and 44, serious amateurs. —Anne Underwood, "Real Rhapsody in Blue," *Newsweek*, December 1, 2003

Like DiOrio, French said she also discovered her synesthesia at an early age. Sitting before the organ for a final rehearsal before her senior recital, French said she was drawn to the instrument because of the wide range of color possibilities it offers. —Catherine Cheney, "It's Not Easy Hearing Green," *Yale Daily News*, September 10, 2008

Synesthesia is formed by the Greek *sun*, "with," and *aisthēsis*, "sensation," and is modeled after *anaesthesia*, literally "without sensation."

syzygy
/(siz'ə-jē)/

noun

1 In *astronomy*, the conjunction or opposition of a planet with the sun, or of any two of the heavenly bodies.
2 In *ancient prosody*, a group or combination of two feet.
3 In *algebra*, a linear function in the variables.
4 In *zoology*, the conjunction of two organs or organisms by close adhesion and partial concrescence, without loss of

their identity; also, the thing so formed, or the resulting conformation.

Examples:

Thus each syzygy (as new and full are technically called) is too early; each quadrature is too late; the maximum hurrying and slackening force being felt at the octants, or intermediate 45° points. —Oliver Lodge, *Pioneers of Science*, 1893

The Assessor sends a "certificate of value" to each following the end of the appeals period on June 30. In turn, they calculate their needs for the fiscal year to come using previous budgets, new projects, windage, periods for lunar syzygy and god-knows-what else. —Morgan Liddick, "Property Taxes Got You Down?" *Summit Daily News*, May 18, 2009

It is the galaxy. Admire also the syzygy of those orbs. —"Courtship of a Vassar Girl," *Prairie Farmer*, January 19, 1884

Syzygy comes from the Greek word *suzugos*, meaning "paired."

109 **tarradiddle**
/(tar'ə did¡l)/

noun
• A fictitious account; a fib.

Examples:

Did I ever tell a lie, Miss Patty? Goodness gracious me! Well, to be sure, perhaps I told a bit of a **tarradiddle** when I was a small child; but an out-and-out lie—never, thank the Almighty! —L. T. Meade, *Girls of the Forest*, 1902

Lady Lufton's **tarradiddle** was of a nature that is usually considered excusable—at least with grown people; but, nevertheless, she would have been nearer to perfection could she have confined herself to the truth. —Anthony Trollope, *Framley Parsonage*, 1861

In vain Kettle pleaded "fo' Gord"—always a forerunner of a **tarradiddle**—that he "didn't have no notion on the blessed yearth as Miss Betty would mind," and also wept copiously when Mrs. Fortescue frankly told him that he was a tarradiddler, and made, for the hundredth time, a very awful threat to Kettle. —Molly Elliot Seawell, *Betty at Fort Blizzard*, 1916

Synonyms for *tarradiddle* include *fib, lie, falsehood, falsity, fiction, fabrication,* and *deception.*

tchotchke

110

/(choch'kə)/

noun

- A small, decorative item or souvenir, usually of no particular value.

Examples:

I've been picking up a multitude of commie tchotchke, especially cheap plastic deskware with pictures of Lenin and Stalin, the hammer and cycle, Red Army symbols, images of war memorials, and more. —Doug Bandow, "The Politics of Collecting," *The Huffington Post*, November 26, 2009

Even with the second-floor tenants and first-floor tchotchke vendors generating $48,000 a year in rent, Fritz has posted either meager profits or moderate losses in recent years, with the rising cost of labor and materials and the downturn in the market. —Annie Groer, "Against the Grain: Keith Fritz Left the Path to the Priesthood to Create Divine Furniture," *The Washington Post*, April 25, 2010

Next month SFMoMA will unveil a line of T shirts, silicon place mats and word puzzles by artist-designer Rex Ray. It's a way of allowing visitors to feel like they're taking home a genuine work of art. But is it really art, or just a gussied-up tchotchke? —Peter Plagens, "Still Life with Beach Towel," *Newsweek*, March 1, 2008

Tchotchke has Yiddish origins.

Terpsichore
/(tûrp-sik'ə-rē)/

proper noun
- In *classical mythology*, one of the Muses, the especial companion of Melpomene, and the patroness of the choral dance and of the dramatic chorus developed from it.

Examples:
Terpsichore is a nymph who practises the Terpsichorean art; indeed, I may say, presides over a number of the arts, for she has the best faro-bank in town, and the only bar where a gentleman can get a drink that will not poison a refined stomach. —Thomas Nelson Page, *Gordon Keith*, 1903

The most stuck-up landowners of the neighborhood rarely fail to make an excursion thither once or twice during the season, arriving at this rustic palace of Terpsichore either in dashing parties on horseback, or in the light and elegant carriages which powder the philosophical pedestrian with dust. —Honoré de Balzac, *The Ball at Sceaux*, 1914

No. Mademoiselle was not engaged either for—or for—or for—&c., &c., &c.; and then out came the little tablets, under the dome of a huge greenhouse filled with the most costly exotics, and Clementina and her fellow-labourer in the cause of Terpsichore went to work to make their arrangements for the evening. —Anthony Trollope, *The Three Clerks*, 1903

Terpsichore comes from the Greek terpsikhoros, "dance-loving."

thropple
/(thrôp'l)/

noun
• The windpipe.

verb
• To throttle; strangle.

Examples:
By the thirst of my thropple, friend, when snow is on the mountains, I say the head and chin, there is not then any considerable heat to be expected in the valleys and low countries of the codpiece. —Francois Rabelais, *Five Books of the Lives, Heroic Deeds and Sayings of Gargantua and His Son Pantagruel*, 1904

The morse is said to roar or bellow loudly, but the animal we slew made no outcry, for the half sneezing, half snorting sounds it uttered I conceive to have been the consequence of its hasty dive, which had apparently prevented its taking in sufficient breath, and occasioned it to admit some water down its windpipe. Nevertheless, the immense size of its larynx or thropple, which William dissected out and brought with him to England, seems to indicate vast powers of voice in this animal . . . —"Arctic Adventures," *The Mirror of Literature, Amusement, and Instruction*, April 25, 1829

The convicted killer would thropple his victims before throwing their bodies in the river. —Wordnik

Thropple is probably an alteration of *throttle*, meaning "the throat" or "to choke."

113   tiddlywinks

/(tĭd'lē-wĭngks̬)/

noun

- A game in which the objective is to shoot winks into a cup or at a target by flicking them with a shooter (nowadays called a squidger) from a surface.

Examples:

At the end, viewers are urged to go to a website, www.spotsvstripes.com, to join a team and compete in any real-life game they like—from tiddlywinks to crazy golf and keepy-uppy—and to build up national totals online for each side. —Mark Sweney, "Cadbury Set to Reveal 2012 Olympics Sponsorship Ads," *The Guardian*, August 2, 2010

His longtime friends say his lust for competition and willingness to gamble on virtually any game—from tiddlywinks to Monopoly—is nothing new. —Mark Starr, "The Gambling Man," *Newsweek*, June 14, 1993

At this point, Clinton and Obama are only circling one another in the ring and jabbing a tentative punch or two. Eventually, it's going to be more than "tiddlywinks and a beanbag"—to quote Obama himself from his interview with Chris Matthews last night on the *Hardball* College Tour. —Mayhill Fowler, "Pennsylvania Campaign Journal: Obama Hams It Up, Flirts, and Gets a Bit Cocky," *The Huffington Post*, April 2, 2008

Tiddlywinks may be a combination of the dialectical word *tiddly*, meaning "little," plus *wink*.

trollop
114

/(trol'əp)/

verb

1 To draggle; hang in a wet state.
2 To walk or work in a slovenly manner.

noun

1 A loose, hanging rag.
2 A woman who is slovenly in dress, appearance, or habits;
a slattern; a draggletail; also, a woman morally loose.

Examples:

Jane obviously wasn't feeling well today; it wasn't like
her to trollop through the office when usually she was so
bright and cheery. —Wordnik

I would like to believe that I am a decent enough human
being to understand that all women, slight and voluptuous, deserve to have representations of feminine beauty
that don't reduce them to mere trollops at the mercy of a
hypersexualized ideal. —Czerina Salud, "Minority Marketing Gone
Wild: Beyond Nivea," *The Huffington Post*, June 26, 2007

Never before has the grip of their "finance" been so evi-
dent, turning families to beggars, brother against brother,
our virtuous girls to commercial trollops, bright children

to noise-sodden acquisitive rebels, students to drug-sodden no-hope wrecks and our race of potential angels to a horde of depraved voracious apes. —"Never Before. Never Again," *OpEdNews.com*, June 12, 2008

Trollop may come from the word *troll*, "to roll about, wallow."

ubiquitous
/(yōō-bik'wi-təs)/

adjective
• Being or existing everywhere; actually or apparently omnipresent: often used in an exaggerated or humorous sense.

Examples:

The improvement in Colombia is something to celebrate. Yet the persistent violence there after decades of sacrifice is troubling. Drugs remain ubiquitous in the U.S. and Europe and demand remains inelastic. —Mary Anastasia O'Grady, "A Stimulus Plan for Mexican Gangsters," *The Wall Street Journal*, March 2, 2009

So ubiquitous is our frustration with junk mail that popculture references to it are increasingly common, the most recent of which was a Saturday Night Live skit featuring a fictional group called "the Alliance of Direct Mail Marketers."

—Todd Paglia, "Junk Mail's Endless Summer," *The Huffington Post*, May 12, 2009

Gaudy 10-foot-high portraits of Saddam Hussein have been touched up with fresh paint. His feared Republican Guard, who monitor occasional roadblocks, are polite and neatly attired. Security forces remain ubiquitous, but surveillance of my movements was light-handed. —"Nothing Left to Lose," *Newsweek*, July 22, 1991

Grid computing uses distributed computers, data storage systems, networks, and other resources as if they were a single massive system. . . . They can be linked up across any network. . . . The presence of major vendors at the Global Grid Forum is a development welcomed by the researchers who together have milled busily to create the next major advance in ubiquitous computing. —"Time to Hop on the Grid-wagon," *Wired*, July 26, 2002

Ubiquitous comes from the Latin word *ubīque*, meaning "everywhere."

(116) verisimilitude

/(ver͵ə-si-mil'i-tōōd͵ *or* ver͵ə-si-mil'i-tyōōd͵)/

noun

1 The quality or state of being verisimilar; the appearance of truth; probability; likelihood: as, the *verisimilitude* of a story.

2 That which is verisimilar; that which has the appearance of a verity or fact.

Examples:

This leads to the important paradox that in the theatre you must be artificial if you wish to appear natural; that on the stage, verisimilitude is greater truth than truth itself; or, to use the popular oxymoron, you must be "falsely true."
—Edward Fordham Spence, *Our Stage and Its Critics*, 1910

Both shows, actually, get mixed marks in verisimilitude from those in the know. White House chief of staff John Podesta seems amused by "The West Wing," but says, "The chief of staff should be younger and meaner-looking."
—"Coast to Coast," *Newsweek*, September 6, 1999

In these times, a writer of either sex attempting to speak as the other is scrutinized for offense. One may venture into the mind of the opposite sex, but verisimilitude is thought to be beyond a writer who attempts to render the physical experience of being the other. —Diane Johnson, "Warlock," *The New York Review of Books*, June 14, 1984

Verisimilitude comes from the Latin word *vērīsimilis*, which is composed of *vērus*, "true," plus *similis*, "similar."

117 vichyssoise
/(vish͵ē-swäz' *or* vē͵shē-swäz')/

noun
- A thick, creamy soup made from potato, leeks, and onions; normally served cold.

Examples:
To achieve a variety of temperatures and textures in this meal, Ms. Cashion suggests serving vichyssoise, a cold potato soup, as a first course. —Joyce Gemperlein, "A Mid-Atlantic Meal," *The Wall Street Journal*, September 15, 2008

As Charles Masson the son tells it, "He was very drunk. He said, 'This vichyssoise is canned.' My father was deeply insulted by the charge. He took my mother over to the senator and said, 'Will you please tell Senator Kennedy how I make the vichyssoise?' And she did, step by step—none of those quick ways he'd learned in Hawaii—at the end of which Robert Kennedy said, 'It's canned.'" —Douglas McGrath, "An Immovable Feast," *Vanity Fair*, September 2008

And for the new rich, who still may be mystified by the difference between a vichyssoise and a vernissage, a pedigreed butler is a godsend. —"You Called For Me, Sir?" *Newsweek*, November 30, 2007

A frothy vichyssoise has a julienne of summer truffle and crème fraîche. —Moira Hodgson, "Dining Out with Moira Hodgson," *The New York Observer*, July 27, 2003

Vichyssoise is named after *Vichy*, a town in Auvergne, France, which was the capital of France during World War II.

whippersnapper
/(hwip'ər-snap͵ər *or* wip' ər-snap͵ər)/

noun

1 A shallow, insignificant person; a whipster: also used attributively.

2 A young and cheeky or presumptuous person.

Examples:

"Why," he turned to Rainey, his voice down-pitching to a growl of angry contempt, "you pen-shovin' **whippersnapper**, I c'ud break you in ha'f with one hand. You ain't her breed. But"—his voice changed again—"if it's a showdown, all right." —J. Allan Dunn, *A Man to His Mate*, 1920

He wanted her to do well, and was upset when she wasn't doing well, and was chafing at this **whippersnapper** Obama, who he doubtless resented both generationally and in the way that many stars resent one another beneath the surface camaraderie of celebrityhood. —William Bradley, "The Last Clinton Melodrama? (And Other Sensationalist *Game Change* Gossip)," *The Huffington Post*, January 14, 2010

But just as the **whippersnapper** is getting revved up, thankfully, someone cuts him off. —Michael Den Tandt, "Name Change Can't Hurt NDP," *Winnipeg Sun*, August 15, 2009

Synonyms for *whippersnapper* include *brat, enfant terrible, gamin, holy terror, imp, malapert, pip-squeak, punk, saucebox, shrimp, squirt, squit, swaggerer, upstart,* and *urchin.*

119 **willy-nilly**
/(wil͵ē-nil'ē)/

adjective
1 Willing or unwilling.
2 Vacillating; shilly-shallying.

Examples:
The hideous period of beginning to begin! I imagine it's like the tense moment in a football game, just before the kickoff, only those lucky youths are pushed and prodded

into action, willynilly. If only a whistle would blow or a pistol crack for me! —Ruth Comfort Mitchell, *Jane Journeys On*, 1922

I do not relish mystery and I detest being led willynilly. —Marie Conway Oemler, *Slippy McGee, Sometimes Known as the Butterfly Man*, 1920

During the 1990s, the Pentagon embarked willy-nilly upon what became its own variant of a settlement policy. —Andrew Bacevich, "The End of (Military) History? The United States, Israel, and the Failure of the Western Way of War," *The Huffington Post*, July 29, 2010

No tricky directorial concepts are sprayed over the text— Mr. Croy is content to let Shakespeare be Shakespeare— and the actors respond by giving of their best, with results that are not merely funny but also emotionally true. Ms. Janson, for instance, is at once heartfelt and touchingly clueless, an innocent flung willy-nilly into the midst of roiling comic chaos. —Terry Teachout, "What's Up, Bard?" *The Wall Street Journal*, August 13, 2009

Willy-nilly is an alteration of "will he or will he not; will ye or will ye not." It is also spelled *willynilly*.

120   **withershins**
/(wi*th*'ər-shinz,)/

adverb
• In the opposite direction; hence, in the wrong way.

Examples:
Arrived at the kirk, they paced around it withershins, that is, in reverse of the apparent motion of the sun. —Charles Mackay, *Memoirs of Extraordinary Popular Delusions*, 1852

To go round a person in the opposite direction, or withershins (German wider-shins), is unlucky, and a sort of incantation. —Sir Walter Scott, *Waverley*, 1814

Osberne made up toward the door, but the carline put forth her hand and thrust him back, and said: "Not yet; abide where thou art a minute;" and straightway fell to going withershins round the house. —William Morris, *The Sundering Flood*, 1814

One very ancient and persistent superstition had regard to the direction of movement either of persons or things. This direction should always be with the course of the sun. To move against the sun was improper and productive of evil consequences, and the name given to this direction of movement was withershins. Witches in their dances and

152

other pranks, always, it was said, went withershins. —James
Napier, *Folk Lore*, 1879

Withershins is Scottish but originally comes from the German *widersinnes: wider,* "back," plus *sinnes,* "in the direction of." It is also spelled *widdershins.*